GW00760833

Being Successful i

Presentations

About the Author

Lynda Byron is a Senior Management Specialist at the Irish Management Institute. She specialises in the areas of personal skills and customer service. She has been designing and delivering much sought after courses on presentations skills for many years.

Lynda's unique style of teaching helps executives at all levels to build confidence and excellence in their skills of presenting by creating a safe and enjoyable learning environment. She helps individuals to realise their own strengths and areas for improvement by giving focused but sensitive feedback.

Being Successful in...
Presentations

Lynda Byron

BLACKHALL
Publishing

This book was typeset by Artwerk for

BLACKHALL PUBLISHING
26 Eustace Street
Dublin 2
Ireland

e-mail: blackhall@tinet.ie

ISBN: 1 901657 56 6

A catalogue record for this book is available from
the British Library.

Printed in Ireland by
Colour Books

Series Foreword

*The Being Successful in...*series is a new series of practical books, which provides an accessible and user-friendly approach to the common problems experienced by small to medium-sized, growing businesses.

The series will help businesses in the start-up phase but also covers problems encountered during the all-important development phase. It will be helpful to businesses which are starting to grow, and which need to cope with a range of unfamiliar, difficult and often competing issues.

The books in the series are comprehensive and yet concise, and they treat the topics in question succinctly and without recourse to jargon. Practical examples, checklists and pointers on to further sources of help and advice are included to supplement the text.

Books published in the *Being Successful in...*series:
Being Successful in...*Report Writing*
Being Successful in...*Customer Care*
Being Successful in...*Budgeting*
Being Successful in...*Patents, Copyright and Trade Marks*

Forthcoming books in the series:

Being Successful in...*Motivation*
Being Successful in...Overcoming Stress
Being Successful in...Public Relations

Contents

Dedication

To Sandra and Sinéad,
of course, and
to Wendy whose courage and
sunny outlook is an inspiration.

Acknowledgements

Thanks to my family and friends who were a constant source of support and encouragement. My colleagues, particularly Frank Byrne and Charles Carroll who read the manuscript and added their infinite wisdom.

To Aoife Lawless, who, with her long experience as a professional actress helped me to understand the power of the voice and how to use it to its best effect.

To my employer, the Irish Management Institute and particularly the rest of the members of the Editorial Board for their help and encouragement.

To Mary Condren who helped me to believe in my writing.

And to Tony Mason, without whose wonderful feedback I would have given up before I even started. He made the onerous job of writing a book seem easy and enjoyable.

Preface: Why You Should Read This Book

This book is for everyone who has to make presentations. It assumes nothing except that you want to improve your skills and make an impact on your audiences.

We all feel differently when faced with the opportunity to present. But this book starts with a very common feeling – fear. This can come in many forms but the best presenters will feel some nerves. This comes from the respect they have for their audiences and actually helps them to make brilliant presentations.

The rest of the book brings you through a structured approach to preparing and delivering presentations with impact, giving you hints and tips as well as tried and tested techniques.

I hope you find it useful.

Lynda Byron
July 1999

Chapter 1

Handling The Fear

This chapter will help you to:

- realise that being nervous is a normal part of presenting;
- see the positive side of nervousness;
- control and hide your nervousness from your audience.

Handling The Fear

The presentation is tomorrow: 10 am sharp. You're talking to the management group, or worse still, the Board. They're unfriendly. You don't know them very well. But you must persuade them. You have to get them to decide on this issue. They must support your idea.

But have you done enough to prepare? Do you know what you're talking about? Do any of them know more than you do on this issue?

Every time you think about it your stomach lurches, your palms sweat – panic is beginning to set in.

Going to bed, you wonder why you bother – you're not going to sleep anyway. You'll toss and turn for hours, picturing their bored or hostile faces as you lie there. Finally you nod off. The shrill alarm wakes you at 8.00 am. But you've only just got to sleep. You suddenly remember what's happening at ten. OH NO! How will you cope? Breakfast – you must be joking!

You drive to the office, grab a coffee and head for the meeting. Standing outside, the shakes start, your scalp is sweating, your stomach is doing somersaults, you feel sick. Your mouth is dry. Why is your tongue sticking to the roof of your mouth? You just know when you start to speak your voice will come out in a quiver. You just want to go home – forget the whole idea. Two weeks ago it seemed like a great opportunity. Wow, presenting to the Board – me! Now all you can see is the wonderful chance of making an absolute fool of yourself.

"Please, please let them cancel the meeting, let me off the hook," you pray. The door opens – the words "You're on," are said. . . Oh God!

Does any of this feel even vaguely familiar? If you have ever presented, I bet it does.

Everyone who makes presentations, no matter how often they do it, no matter how good they are, no matter what level they are in the company feel nervous before making a presentation. That's if they're any good. It's normal, it's OK, it's necessary. If you're not nervous you can't possibly perform well as a presenter.

There is a positive and a negative side of nerves. Nerves get the adrenaline going. When the adrenaline starts pumping around your body, different things happen. The negative side is what we're all too familiar with: butterflies in the stomach, sweating, shaking, twitches, stuttering, dry mouth, wobbly voice, red rash that rises from the neck up through the face and all the rest. I guarantee you've felt a large proportion of them yourself. You can control these and you must. More of that later.

The positive side is less obvious to the presenter but very obvious to the audience. As the adrenaline pumps you get energy. This energy encourages your enthusiasm and passion. A presenter who is lethargic, lacks energy and enthusiasm, doesn't seem to care about the subject, is boring to listen to, appears to be "going through the motions".

A presenter, on the other hand, who is nervous but is controlling the nerves well, is interesting, exciting and easy to listen to. Which would you rather be?

FACING THE FEAR

Ask yourself what are you really afraid of? What is the worst thing that can happen? Below are some common answers to these questions.

- Making a fool of myself.
- The equipment breaking down.
- Not being able to answer questions.
- Hostile audiences.
- Being in the limelight – all the focus is on me.
- Making a bad impression.
- Panicking when I look at the audience.
- Jokes going flat.
- Boring the audience.
- If I make a bad presentation, my boss will think I can't do my job either.

All of these fears can be handled by preparing your presentation meticulously, checking your equipment carefully and delivering with skill. The rest of this book looks at how you can avoid the above pitfalls and learn these skills. Presenting is a learned skill. There is no reason why anybody can't make a good presentation once they are prepared to put the work into it. But first you need to manage yourself so that you avoid the worst symptoms of nerves being shown to your audience.

CONTROLLING YOUR NERVES

Being nervous is good, in fact it is essential for any good presenter but you must control your nerves. Usually, if you are well prepared, the worst effects of nerves subside after the first few minutes of a presentation, because you will have already started to get a positive response from the audience and know you are going to do well. There are numerous ways you can help yourself. Here are a few.

Imagine yourself Succeeding

All too often when we are asked to make a presentation, we imagine all the pitfalls, the things that can and will inevitably go wrong. Why not picture yourself in front of that group of people looking confident, smiling, in control. Is that so hard? When I first started presenting, I used to be afraid of the audience reaction. I was so afraid that they'd feel sorry for me. I couldn't bear to think of their pitiful faces, saying to themselves: "Ah God love her, she's very nervous." That was my worst night-

> **WORD TO THE WISE**
> If you appear confident and seem to be enjoying the presentation, it is highly likely that your audience will enjoy listening to you.

mare. You may have a different bad dream in your mind. I now picture all the groups I talk to as having happy, smiling faces. They're all enjoying the presentation, they're all interested. That's what keeps me going. If you appear confident and seem to be enjoying the presentation, it is highly likely that your audience will enjoy listening to you. Think of things you do well, the things you're really good at. Try and capture the feelings you get when you're succeeding at that activity and transpose them onto your presentation. Try it, it's not as far-fetched as you think.

Think of your Audience as Friendly, not Hostile

Think about how you feel when you are a member of an audience. Are you hoping that the presenter will die on their feet or do you hope they will be interesting? Usually an audience is hoping for a good presentation. They're not automatically hostile. In fact, sometimes the audience is almost as nervous as you, they may be asked a question that they can't answer or to make a decision and are hoping you'll give them enough information for them to make it well. Give them the benefit of the doubt. Remember your behaviour can influence theirs. If you behave as though you're confident and enjoying yourself, they'll expect you to make an excellent presentation. If you look nervous and worried, they may expect you to get it wrong.

Certainly there may be one or two people in your audience who may be hostile towards you. Try to work out who they may be in advance and why. It is possible that they don't feel that you should have been asked to present at all, maybe they feel they should have been asked. You need to flatter these people in front of the rest of the audience and make them feel good about you being up there. You need to turn them around. In Chapter 7, you will find some tips on handling some of these hostile behaviours.

Relax, Chill Out

Deep breathing can help you while you're waiting for your turn to present. Ensure you're breathing from your whole chest, taking in deep breaths and letting them out slowly. Take a few minutes on your own just before you start. Leave the room, find a quiet corner and contemplate your navel for five minutes. Go over your opening lines and try to remember what you're going to say next. This will give you more confidence. Now you're ready to face the group.

Beating the Shakes

When the adrenaline starts pumping in advance of a presentation, it can cause a trembling in your body. This can be at its worst in your hands. Everyone can see you tremble. Everything you pick up seems to wobble everywhere. You try to drink a glass of water to calm you down and you spill it all down your front. You drop your notes and slides all over the floor. The red dot of your laser pointer runs all over the screen. This is one of the most visible aspects of the negative side of nervousness and is something you must control as it is an instant give-away.

If your hands are shaking, avoid holding pieces of paper, slides or cards in your hands as these make your hand appear larger and the shake more exaggerated. Leave paper down on a side table and only pick up slides when you need to use them. When you're changing slides on the overhead projector hold them firmly with two hands. This will stop them wobbling, and do everything with very definite and obvious movements. This will make you appear more confident.

We often need to point at particular figures on a slide, if your hands are shaking don't use your finger to point as it will show up on the screen as a gigantic, out of control thing. Instead, try placing a pen down on the slide, using that same definite movement to point to the relevant spot. Make sure the pen has a clip or square edges so that it doesn't roll off the overhead projector and make it even more awkward for you. The same goes for the infrared remote control with an LCD presentation, be careful not to leave your finger on the button which changes slides. If you are shaky, you are likely to change the slides by mistake, rushing past two or three slides at a time. The audience will notice this. So keep your finger off the button when you're not actually using it.

What about those legs? Did you ever get a wobble in one knee that you can't seem to stop? There it is, knee shaking like crazy and your foot leaping about all over the place for all to see. Try shaking out your knees before you go into the room to help relax them and keep walking around. Remember it is only when you stand still that your knees will shake.

Wipe Out the Trembling Voice

You have your opening line all worked out, well

prepared, meticulously rehearsed and then you look at the audience and all that comes out is a little wobbly voice "Good morning everyone" that no one can hear and destroys any last shred of confidence you may have left. How can you possibly go on after that? This hasn't really made the impact you had intended. Luckily, there is a very simple solution to this common problem. If you say your first line loudly – boom it out, you'll find that not only will it grab the attention of your audience, it is also a physical impossibility for your voice to tremble, there is just too much force behind it. It will have the added advantage of making you feel in control and in command of your audience. There are also numerous voice exercises you can try which will help you to feel more confident about your voice (see Chapter 6).

Dry Mouth

Sufferers from dry mouth will experience an uncomfortable time while they're talking. Your tongue will be sticking to the roof of your mouth, your lips will be like sandpaper and welded together and your gums itchy. Sounds lovely. When we feel this coming on we usually reach for a glass of water to try and lubricate the mouth as quickly as possible. This can be dangerous when you're standing in front of a group. It's a bit like trying to drink a glass of water after you've just been to the dentist for a filling. You are likely to miss your mouth altogether and pour the liquid all down your front, which is all you need.

An altogether safer remedy is to conjure up a picture in your mind. While you're reading this, imagine you're going to the fridge and taking out a big, juicy lemon. You're putting this down on a chopping board on a nearby worktop and cutting it down the middle with a sharp knife. The juice is flooding out of the lemon onto the board. Now, pick up one half of the lemon and squeeze the juice into a glass. Are you salivating? If this is working for you now, it will also work during a presentation. Once you've done it once, all you need is the picture of the lemon in your mind to bring back the memory of the juice and you will be drooling in no time. No more dry mouth problems.

Creeping, Red Rash

Many women, particularly, complain of this. Red blotches which start on their chest and creep up their neck and finally onto their faces. If you are a sufferer, always make sure you are wearing a high neck blouse or a shirt with a scarf in the neck. This will cover the rash for a while and hopefully just knowing that your audience can't see your embarrassment will be enough to make it subside before it reaches the facial area. If, however, it has a habit of continuing its journey above the jawline, then invest in some make-up with a slight green tinge. Your local beautician or pharmacy will advise you on the best one for you.

REMEMBER

DO:

- Face your fears – we all have them.
- Capitalise on your nerves by using them to make an energetic presentation.
- Learn to manage your nerves.

DO NOT:

- Worry about being nervous – it's a good thing.
- Assume the audience is out to get you.
- Think you'll be a star without putting in the work.

Chapter 2

Building Credibility

This chapter will help you to:

- understand why credibility is important in a speaker;
- see how you can become an expert;
- learn to be yourself;
- work on your image.

Building Credibility

Imagine yourself in DIY mode at home. You've been intending to put a set of shelves on the wall in the kitchen for months now and finally you've decided that today is the day. The shelves are lying on the floor, the drill is out of the box on the kitchen table but you don't know which type of screws to use. So it's off to the local DIY store for advice. At the counter, you explain your problem to Charlie. You have three shelves, 3 foot long and 5 inches wide. You have bought wrought-iron brackets but you need advice on which screws you need to fix them to the wall. The scruffy assistant looks at you vaguely, shakes his head, scratches his chin and mumbles distractedly, "Weeeeelllll, you could try these ones, or maybe these would be better...I suppose these will do you." He hands you a packet of pre-packed steel screws. Do you think you've got good advice? Would you do what he suggests or would you seek a second opinion. I'd be inclined to ask someone else, after all he didn't look or sound very confident, did he?

As a contrast, think about an assistant in another hardware store, Jimmy, when you ask him the same question. He is smartly dressed, casual but clean and tidy. He smiles when you approach him. He asks a few questions to get the necessary information first (such as, "What type of wall are you attaching them to?"; "What will you be putting on the shelves?"; "What tools do you have to do the job?"). When he has collected all the information, he says, in a confident voice, "If I were doing that job, I'd use these screws with these rawlplugs, you can't go wrong." Would you feel more confident with this approach? I bet you would.

What makes Jimmy credible and Charlie not credible? Jimmy is an expert. He has personal experience of putting up shelves – he told you as much. He looks confident, he sounds confident, he is confident. He has done his homework. He knows his stuff. Charlie has probably never put up shelves in his life. He doesn't know what he's doing. He looks and sounds as though he is making it up, as though he can't be trusted.

There is a similarity between the above example and a presenter. I'm sure you've watched a presentation where the speaker is vague, doesn't seem to know what he or she is talking about and stumbles through even the simplest of explanations. The impression they give is unprofessional and not credible. Usually this puts us off and stops us from taking them seriously.

How do you come across? Do you always do your homework? Are you an expert in your subject? You need to be. Would you prefer to be a Charlie or a Jimmy?

If we are listening to a Charlie-type presenter, we don't always believe what they are saying to us. We feel irritated by them. We sometimes get hostile because we feel that Charlie doesn't have enough respect for us to bother coming prepared. We don't respect him because he doesn't appear to respect us. We are more likely to ask difficult questions to expose this unprofessional speaker. Remember, people buy people. If we want our audience to listen to what we're saying, we need to show them we really care about them.

> **WORD TO THE WISE**
> Be an expert, look like an expert...People like to think they're listening to an expert.

If you want to build credibility with your audience, you must both become an expert and appear to be an expert.

BE AN EXPERT

You need to start by doing your homework. Find out all you can about your subject. Read around the topic, ask lots of people, try things out, experience as much as you can. All of this will give you confidence and make you more of an expert.

You may be often asked to speak about a subject you feel you are an expert in. This is good – look for these opportunities and take all of them. But you must prepare very well even if you know all there is to know (see Chapter 3).

Sometimes, however, we are asked to speak about a topic that is a little alien to our background or line of work. If it is something you can find out about and you have the time to do your homework, that's okay. Work hard at becoming very knowledgeable on the subject and you'll be fine. If you are asked to make one of these presentations tomorrow...refuse. When you don't have the time to research properly, you are doomed to fail. You're only setting yourself up to make a show of yourself. Don't fall into this trap.

There are other subjects which you will never be able to get to grips with no matter how much time you have and no matter how hard you try. These are other times when you should refuse. You were probably asked because someone has heard you speak on your pet subject and you were brilliant. This does not mean that you can be brilliant on any topic. It is flattering to be asked, but if you can't do it well, you shouldn't even try.

The main message, therefore, is if you're happy that you can be an expert you should take the opportunity to present. If you cannot be knowledgeable on the topic, then leave it to someone else. Don't let yourself be talked into presenting on a subject that you don't feel comfortable with – it will only damage your credibility and your confidence. If you can match their needs with your strengths, you're in business. It's a question of fit.

In the last chapter, we spoke about having passion for your subject, this passion is an essential part of being a good presenter. If you are passionate about a subject, take as many opportunities that come your way to present on it. You will build your credibility as a speaker in this way.

But don't forget, nobody knows everything about a subject. Nobody is expecting you to know everything. If you are asked a question that you can't answer, be honest and say so. It is quite legitimate to tell your enquirer that you hadn't thought about that aspect before and would they mind if you checked it up and got back to them. Usually this makes them feel good that they thought of a question that the 'expert' hadn't even considered before and if you handle them sensitively they will admire your honesty and your real enthusiasm for your subject. By the way, if you say you will get back to them, be sure you do.

BE YOURSELF

Be yourself when presenting. You have all seen wonderful presenters in action who command the attention of the audience effortlessly. You would love to be like them; unruffled, confident, in control. They look and sound good. You wonder if you could ever be like them. A mistake which presenters often make is trying to mimic other good presenters. You must be yourself. You have huge strengths – use them to your advantage. If you try to be like someone else, you will lose your strengths and you probably won't be able to mimic their good parts well enough so, ultimately, you'll lose credibility with your audience because you look, and sound, like a fake.

Everyone can be a good presenter. It is a learned skill. I don't believe it is a skill we're born with. Learn what your strengths are and find out what your little problems are so that you can correct them. You can be a good presenter if you are willing to put the work into it. Certainly it comes a little more naturally to some than others.

> **WORD TO THE WISE**
> Don't ever try to present like someone you admire. Be yourself. Otherwise, the audience will see through you.

There are only a select few who can be brilliant, charismatic presenters, but all of us can be professional, interesting and credible.

LOOK THE PART

How do people perceive you? How would you like to be perceived by your audience?

Imagine yourself sitting in a pub, chatting to a friend. The door opens and in walks a man who is dressed a little strangely, maybe has long hair, very loud coloured clothes, big boots. You see him walking past you while there is a lull in the conversation. Think about your reaction. Usually what we do is to pass a remark to our friend, "Who's your man? He's weird!" Now, think about what made you say that. You don't know this man or anything about him. You don't actually know he's weird. All you know about him is that he is dressed a little strangely. What you have just done is to make a judgement about a person by the way he is dressed.

Audiences do this en masse. Everything that the audience can see of you can help them make up their minds about whether you're credible or not. They will look at your clothes, your hair, your shoes and if they're close enough will even look at your fingernails.

Your grooming and dress need to be appropriate

to the audience and to the image you want to portray. Usually a good rule of thumb is that you should be at least as well dressed as the best-dressed person in the room. This shows respect for the audience. For example, if you are presenting to a group of business people, it would be appropriate to wear a suit. But here you have to be careful. If you never wear a suit because you are, for example, an artistic type of person working in that line of work, a business suit may be the wrong choice. In which case a smart version of your 'artistic' clothes would be more appropriate.

Some invitations to speak bear the instructions 'dress casual'. Watch out, this is dangerous. Dress casual to you may mean jeans and a jumper but to someone else, who may be in your audience, it may just mean not wearing their best tie. If in doubt, always err on the side of dressing up rather than down. If you turn up to a presentation in a suit and discover that all of your audience are in casual clothes, it is very easy to take off the jacket and tie, loosen the collar of the shirt and roll up your sleeves. Now you're casual – just like them. It is, however, impossible to turn jeans and a jumper into a smart suit, no matter how hard you try.

It is important to see yourself as your audience will see you. Sometimes seeing yourself on video can help with this. You get used to seeing yourself in the mirror in that crumpled suit with your hair a little too long and specks of mud on your shoes. You don't notice these little things any more. Recording yourself on video even for a few minutes can be very revealing. It is something I notice when I work with groups of managers. When they see themselves on video the first thing they notice is the fact that they need a haircut or that their shirt is hanging out. It helps us to see ourselves as others do.

Don't fall into the trap of rushing out to buy a new outfit for a presentation and wear it for the first time standing in front of one hundred people. That's the wrong time to discover that there is an itchy label that is tearing the skin off your neck every time you move. It is also too late to discover that the hem hasn't been stitched properly and is hanging down for all to see. Try to wear the outfit in advance to make sure all is well and it really does look as smart as it is intended to. The same goes for shoes. It is hard to be persuasive when your feet are killing you and your new shoes are squeeking.

Clothes can be distracting. If you want the audience to remember you and what you're saying rather than your fashion sense, avoid wearing an outrageously coloured tie or a loud suit. Wear something that is professional, smart and won't take away from what you're saying. Patterns make you blink. Every time you blink, it takes away from your brain's concentration on the topic. Don't buy fabrics that will shine under bright lights. A subtle pattern like a light pin stripe is fine in a fabric with a matt finish.

Different colours say different things about you. A black suit may make you look extremely authoritative but it may also give the impression that you are arrogant and power-hungry. A better selection would be dark navy or dark grey with a crisp white or pale blue shirt and a smart tie.

However, your image will only help you at the start of your presentation. If you look awful and make a wonderful presentation, you will still be rated much more highly than if you look great and make a terrible presentation.

A SPECIAL WORD FOR WOMEN

It is a little more difficult for a woman to look authoritative but always possible through the right selection of clothes, shoes and make-up. Don't feel you have to 'power-dress'. It is not essential or even desirable to dress like a man. Women should always wear a tailored suit when presenting if they want to appear professional. Knitted suits, cardigans, knitted waistcoats just don't have the same effect. Navy, or dark grey suits with pretty, not over-fussy blouses or shirts look smart and neat. Watch out for anything that is frilly, this can create the wrong impression. Don't overdo the jewellery either. A simple brooch, small earrings and a plain chain around the neck are sufficient. Any more might be distracting.

Make-up should look natural and not overdone and comfy shoes are a must. A small heel can help to boost your confidence and help you to look smarter but don't wear great big heels to make you appear taller, you could find it difficult to move quickly enough. Remember, when we get nervous, we also get clumsy. You really don't want to fall off your shoes in front of a group of people, it tends to take the credibility away a little.

REMEMBER

DO:

- Your homework – be an expert.
- Decide what image you want to portray.
- Show respect for your audience by how you look and by preparing well.

DO NOT:

- Present on a topic you're not comfortable with.
- Wear uncomfortable or distracting clothes.

Chapter 3

Preparation Is The Key

This chapter will help you to:

- set clear objectives;
- tailor your presentation to your audience;
- arrange your content for effect;
- rehearse for the big day.

Preparation Is The Key

SETTING REALISTIC OBJECTIVES

Remember when you were at school or college and exams were coming up? The teachers or lecturers would beat into you that you must first read, then answer the question and you shouldn't waffle all around the topic or just write all you know about the general subject area. You must show the examiner not only that you know the subject, but that you understand it well enough to be able to answer a specific question on it.

What did we do? Most of us, at any rate, decided to ignore the good advice of our teachers and put everything but the kitchen sink into the answer. The poor examiners had to work extremely hard to distil out of our answer what we were really trying to say. And we wondered why we didn't do so well when the results came out. Our friends who did brilliantly probably didn't write nearly so much, but wrote what the examiner wanted to read. They answered the question.

There is a huge similarity between taking exams and making presentations – even apart from the nerves. Your audience has certain expectations when they come along to listen to you. They want to get something out of your presentation. If you want to be successful you must find out what that is.

So, you've been asked to make a presentation in two weeks' time. Your first task is to sit down quietly somewhere with a blank sheet of paper and a pen and write down clearly your objectives for the presentation.

ASK YOURSELF THE FOLLOWING QUESTIONS

- Why am I making this presentation?

- What am I trying to achieve?

- What do I want to have in my audience's head as they leave the room?

- How do I want them to feel?

- What do I want them to do as a result of my presentation?

If you can't answer the above questions, then go back to the person who briefed you and ask them to clarify your purpose. You cannot possibly make an effective presentation without knowing first what your outcome needs to be.

About ten years ago, I was responsible for selling a series of products. They were products which needed to be sold nationwide and in large volume. I decided that as I was good at making sales presentations, I would do my selling that way. It would get me to a large market relatively easily. I invited large groups of personnel and training managers, who were my potential customers, to attend my presentations and worked out what I was going to say to them. I was surprised at the numbers of people who were interested in attending and delighted at the interest they appeared to show on the night.

However, I was disappointed in the number of sales. I knew I had made a good presentation, but why weren't they all queuing up to buy from me? It didn't make sense until I realised that I had set an unrealistic objective. They weren't the sort of products that you could sell en masse. Personnel and training managers needed time to make up their minds as to the suitability of the products, they also needed to talk through the relevance of the products to their own needs. I had to rethink my objectives for the presentation. I began to realise that, although my overall objectives were still the same (to sell the products), the objectives for the actual presentation itself had to be different. The new objectives that I set were to:

- raise awareness of the product;
- let managers know that we were distributing this product;
- get managers to set up an appointment for me to visit them.

Not only were these objectives more realistic but, by being very aware of them before I started putting the content together, it meant that everything I said was leading the audience where I wanted them to go.

WHO IS YOUR AUDIENCE?

Once you've set solid objectives, the next step is to think hard about your audience. There should be no such thing as a standard presentation that you deliver to every group of people. All presentations need to be tailored for the specific audience you're talking to in order for it to work effectively.

WORD TO THE WISE
All presentations need to tailored to the specific audience they are aimed at in order to be effective.

Again, look at the set of questions given below.

- Who is your audience?
- What are their interests?
- What are they expecting to hear?
- What do they want to hear?
- Are they business people or not?

- If so, what level are they at – more senior to me, junior to me?
- Are they male or female?
- What profession are they in: accountants, solicitors, engineers, doctors?
- What functional areas do they work in – marketing, production, general management?
- What will excite them and get them thinking "this sounds interesting"?
- What do they know about this topic?
- How many of them will be there?

It sounds like a lot of questions, but they will help you enormously when you're trying to connect with your audience. The best presentations are relevant to the audience because people will only really listen to a presenter if they think they're talking about something that's relevant to them. So the more homework you can do the better.

If you don't know enough about your audience, go back to the person who briefed you and find out. If you're going to talk to a potential customer company, get on the internet and see what you can find out there. Ask around, what work have they done recently, what work do they specialise in. Have they upsized, downsized, remained static? Have they been in the newspapers recently? If so, why? Get some history as well as current information. How long have they been in business? Who founded the company and is that person still involved? Are they part of a multinational, if so, how big is the company worldwide? How important is the local operation? Will there be other nationalities at the presentation? If so, what language do they speak, other than English.

If you are speaking to a sports club, find out how they're doing recently. What competitors have they been up against? How did they do? How many teams, or equivalent, do they have?

If you are talking to a group of employees in your own company, this research is just as important. You need to know what is currently at the forefront of their minds, what are they thinking about at the moment. Your topic may not be the most pressing matter in their minds, you need to tie your presentation in to their current problems and issues so that they feel you are worth listening to. At the very least you must know what is important to them.

All this information is vital in order to impress your audience. If you can include facts and figures about the audience you are talking to, they will be very impressed and feel flattered that you went to the trouble to find out about them. When people feel flattered, they tend to be impressed with their flatterers.

When you have worked out what your objectives are and done your homework on your audience, you can then start thinking about your content. Unfortunately, this is where most presenters start and they wonder why their audience has gone to sleep.

The only content you should include in any presentation is that which will bring this particular audience towards the objective you have set for yourself. Anything else should be left out. Remember the exam question? This is the most painful part, having to leave out information which you find interesting or that you spent hours, weeks or even months putting together. It may be interesting to you but if it is not going to interest your audience and bring them where you want to take them, it is waffle. Leave it out!

COLLECTING IT ALL TOGETHER

Collecting your content is a vital part of the process. When you know you have a presentation to make, maybe in a few weeks, take a big brown envelope or a manila file, put the name of the presentation on it and leave it on the corner of your desk where you will see it every day. Every time you have an idea for content or find out anything about your target audience, scribble it down and put it in the envelope. Most of us have no problem having good ideas but when we are trying to pull them all together into a shape, we often forget them. If you have captured them all in the same place you'll find it easier to arrange them later.

You may have noticed that you don't have your best ideas when you're sitting at your desk. Most of us don't unless we work in a very creative environment. We all have ideas in different places. If you don't know your most creative places, you should find out. Some typical ones are out walking the dog, digging the garden, in the loo, driving the car, lying in bed or taking a shower. You'll notice a common denominator in all these.

It's hard to capture the ideas. That's one of the reasons you can be so creative. You're not trying to have an idea. You're busy doing something you enjoy, something relaxing. You need to work out your best 'ideas place' and work out a way of capturing those ideas. Try carrying around a small hardbacked notebook and pen, a dictaphone or a mobile phone. I've tried them all and they all work. The mobile phone is great at weekends, when an idea hits me, I ring my office voicemail and leave a message for myself for Monday morning. When I get to the office, I simply listen to my message (I know its horrible listening to a message from yourself, but if it works for you, you'll get over it!), jot it down on a piece of paper and put it into the envelope.

ARRANGING YOUR MATERIAL

About a week before the big day, you should take your envelope full of relevant bits and pieces and start putting a shape on what you are going to say. Keep your objectives beside you while you're doing this so you don't go charging off in the wrong direction. You must stay focused.

There is no standard way to arrange an effective presentation. It will depend entirely on your individual style, your audience and what you are trying to achieve. There are, however, some tips in the next chapter for capturing and holding attention which you shoud bear in mind when putting it all together.

At this stage, you will have to decide how you will remember what you are going to say. I would advise strongly against reading from a written script. It is very hard to hold the attention of your audience in this way unless you have a professional script writer. The audience doesn't see enough of you. You can't look at them, you're static and your script is rigid.

A much better way of going about it is to have a series of headings and sub-headings that you will talk around. Rehearse what you're going to say for each section but don't rely on it all being written down in front of you. Another problem of writing out a full speech is that we write in written English but speak in conversational English. Written English tends to be more formal, and uses longer words and sentences. This is more difficult for an audience to listen to, and usually sounds contrived.

If you want to write out your full script, translate it into conversational English afterwards and then go through it with a highlighter pen and underline the key points. This will help you to shape your thoughts as well as remember what you're going to say.

REHEARSE, REHEARSE, REHEARSE!

All good presenters rehearse. I know you'll feel a proper wally standing in front of the mirror talking away to yourself, but it'll help you enormously with your delivery if you have gone through what you're going to say a few times in advance. If you watch any really good presenter, they make it sound as though they're having ideas off the top of their heads and thinking about how to get them across as they're saying them. Don't be fooled, this is not usually the case. Those really good presenters have probably rehearsed all those ad libs over and over again until they sound just right.

You can rehearse wherever you like but you should try to have at least one rehearsal using all of the notes and audio-visual aids that you will be using on the day. For informal presentations, particularly regular ones that don't make you too nervous, this will probably be enough. If, however, you are making a formal, once-off presentation to a large group of people, you would be better to try and rehearse in the conference room or hall where you will be performing as well. You will need to work out where to stand, where to put your notes so you'll be able to see them easily, how you are going to get on and off the stage easily.

The reason I mention this point especially is that this is where I came unstuck when speaking at a large conference a few years ago. I had even gone along to rehearse with the other speakers the night before bringing my slides and notes. The rehearsal had gone well, very well in fact. I felt good, nervous but confident, the next morning when I turned up in my glad rags, all ready for my big moment. Although I had meticulously rehearsed my content the night before, I hadn't thought about how to get on and off the podium. I know it sounds silly but the night before I was wearing jeans and runners.

Now I was in a tight skirt and shoes with a heel. All the rest of the speakers were men with long legs. Anyone who knows me will know that I am not a tall person. I was doing fine until I tried to step delicately onto the podium and realised that there was no step – this was no problem in jeans, but turned out to be a major problem in a tight skirt. Try as I might I couldn't get up, so there was nothing else for it but to hoist up the skirt and jump – and this in front of 200 people. That would have been okay except that as I was jumping I could hear a ripping noise, the seam at the back of my skirt had started to part company. All through my presentation, the only thing I could think of was how was I going to get back down to my seat without the entire audience seeing my ripped skirt. The moral of this story is rehearse every aspect of your presentation. Try to cater for every eventuality and you will find that less things will go wrong.

REMEMBER

DO:

- Set clear objectives before you start.
- Find out all you can about your audience.
- Give yourself time to rehearse.

DO NOT:

- Include topics in your presentation that won't interest your audience.
- Set unrealistic objectives.

Chapter 4

Grabbing And Holding Attention

This chapter will help you to:

- grab the attention of your audience;
- make your presentation relevant to each of them;
- make your audience remember your key points.

Grabbing And Holding Attention

The first minute of any presentation is where the audience will make a decision as to whether or not you're worth listening to. So you have to make an impact during this first minute or you've lost them. Presenters who start limply with "Hello, my name is Joe Bloggs and I'm here to talk to you about…" are likely to lose their audience before they even start. They're not saying anything that will attract the audience's attention. They're not waking them up. They sound boring.

Equally important is the end of your presentation. You will often hear speakers finishing with an innocuous line, such as, "Well, that's all I have to tell you about that, I think that's it." How exciting, how absolutely riveting. The problem is that the audience will remember most of what was said during the last minute, particularly if the speaker has said one of the key finishing phrases a minute from the end "…and finally", "…and just to summarise", "…to pull it all together", "…in conclusion". Have you ever noticed how an audience reacts when one of these phrases is used? Everyone sits up and starts to get interested again. All the people who were asleep or thinking about other more important issues will suddenly straighten up in their chairs and listen for the next minute. Don't waste this minute. You have everyone's undivided attention. Make the most of it.

What I have been describing above are two psychological phenomena called 'primacy' and 'recency'. We tend to remember most about the first thing that happens and the last thing that happens. To illustrate this point, let me give you two examples. Take a situation you may be in socially. You have decided to go to a restaurant on a Saturday night.

It is a restaurant you've been to once before about six months ago. You know it's a lovely place and the food was good last time so you feel confident that you and your partner will enjoy the evening.

You reserve a table for 8.00 pm. You arrive at exactly the right time. As you're standing by the door, the head waiter seems to look straight through you. You're not getting much attention. In fact nobody has even come near you. You begin to feel embarrassed but realise that he is busy so you wait patiently. After a few minutes of being ignored, the door opens again and another couple come in behind you. The head waiter sees them immediately and waves them into the restaurant with a big smile, leaving you standing by the door. Finally, after another few minutes, he comes over to you with a strained face and says coolly, "follow me", and shows you to a table beside the door to the gent's toilets. By now you are feeling pretty bad about the restaurant and are likely to be looking for any fault you can find to complain about. If there is a stain on the table cloth, you will notice it. If the service is slow, you will get angry. If the food is cold or not well cooked, you will be livid. In other words, if the start of a service encounter is not good, you'll be looking for more problems.

What about the opposite situation. You arrive at the same restaurant and as you come in through the door, the head waiter is immediately over to you welcoming you like a long lost friend. "Good evening, it's lovely to see you again," he says as he shows you to a lovely table just beside the window. Now you've been made to feel a little special. If there is a stain on the table cloth, you are likely to put the salt cellar on top of it rather than complain about it. You will hardly notice if the service is slow and if the meal isn't the best you may decide that you come here for the atmosphere, not the food. The start of the service encounter has again coloured your view of the entire evening.

You may at some time have been involved in recruitment interviewing. If you are interviewing a few people for the same job, you will have noticed that as you interview the first one you pay a lot of atten-

WORD TO THE WISE
Always open and close your presentation with a bang.

tion to him or her. They are the first one, after all. You are fresh. The second candidate comes in through the door and you immediately start measuring them against the previous candidate. The third and fourth candidates appear and you do the same, always measuring against the first candidate. The last person comes along and because they are the last and final candidate you start paying attention again. You may also notice that when you're sitting down after all the interviewees are gone, you can remember most about the first and last candidates. This is known as the primacy and recency effect. If all else is equal, the first or last candidate stand the best chance of getting the job. The first candidate sets the standard against which all the others will be measured and you will be able to remember most about the last one because they were the most recent.

The same principles apply to presentations. If you really want to make an impact on your audience you need to pay particular attention to the start and end of your presentation.

START WITH A BANG

What this means is simply thinking about your audience and making sure that you start with something they will be interested in. Try telling them something they don't already know. Give them an interesting statistic, talk to them about something that is uppermost in their mind. Remember this is the point where they are deciding whether they will stay awake and listen to you or not. Make it worth their while to stay with you. Make your presentation sound as though they can't possibly miss it. Make it exciting.

ADD A MEMORABLE ENDING

You need to remind your audience what you've been talking about within the last few minutes or so. Then give them something definite to think about or do as a result of what you've been saying. Your last sentence should reflect your objectives. This is what is going to be in your audience's head as they leave.

But what about the body of the presentation. How do you make that interesting? Have you ever talked to a colleague and decided that you'd both like to attend a talk some afternoon but only one of you can. Your colleague goes along. You meet that evening and ask her how the presentation went. She said it was great, very interesting, pity you couldn't go as well. But when you asked her what the speaker said, she couldn't remember anything. This often happens, the presenter entertains but their points are not memorable. How can you make sure that your audience will remember what you've said? For a start you must make it relevant to them but secondly you must try to think about the way they are communicating.

THREE COMMUNICATION CHANNELS

According to John Townsend,[1] we all work on three different communication channels. These are:

- **V**isual;
- **H**earing;
- **F**eeling.

All of us use all three to communicate but most of

---

1. Townsend, *The Business Presenter's Pocketbook* (Management Pocketbooks: 1985) p. 28.

us have a preferred channel which we use more easily and regularly. Take, for instance, a situation where a friend asks you for directions to your house. How are you likely to give those directions? A visual person will draw a map, it may not be a great map but at least it's visual. A hearing person will give specific directions like first right, second left, right at the T junction and fourth turn on the left. A person working on the feeling channel as a preference will be more likely to say things like "remember that pub we had a pint in last week, the one on the corner, well turn right there, then you go to the church where Pat and Sheila got married and turn left there, then its right at the T junction where the green is in front of you", etc.

If you listen to different people speaking, you'll notice that we use quite different words and phrases to express ourselves.[2]

Visual Phrases

- I see what you mean.
- We're going to have to look closely at this idea.
- Why don't I look into this and get back to you.
- I can't quite visualise how it'll work.
- What are your views on this?

Hearing Phrases

- I hear what you're saying.
- Tell me more about that.
- I don't like the sound of this.
- That went in one ear and out the other.

Feeling Phrases

- I'll be in touch with you soon.
- I have a gut feeling about this.
- This doesn't feel right to me.

2. McDermott & O'Connor, *Practical NLP for Managers* (Gower: 1996) p. 149.

- I can't put my finger on what's wrong.

We all use these phrases from time to time, but if you find yourself using one type rather than the others, then it'll give you a good idea which communication channel is your preference. Your audience will be made up of a mixture of people with the different preferences. In order to really grab the attention of each of them, you need to ensure you are explaining each point in three different ways. This will also mean that each audience member will get each key point three times. This will help them to remember your all-important messages.

For further evidence of this, Edgar Dale, a researcher, developed what is now known as 'Dale's Cone of Experience'. He says people will remember:

- 20 per cent of what they hear.
- 30 per cent of what they see.
- 50 per cent of what they see and hear.
- 80 per cent of what they hear, see and do.

For each key point, try to tell your audience what you need to tell them, using evidence, key facts and figures. Show them what you mean by using visuals, props, illustrations, etc. Then tell them stories, give them examples to help them to feel how they could use the information you're giving them. If you can get them involved in some way by getting them to help you work through a real example, it will be even more powerful.

MAKE IT RELEVANT

Your audience will be most interested in the parts of your presentation that are directly relevant to them.

You may have noticed what encourages you to listen. Usually anything which has an impact on your life, your job, your family, your earnings, your future, in fact any issue of importance to you.

Talk directly to your audience, don't put them in the third party, this will make them think you're talking to someone else and it will lose its relevance.

For instance, if you are trying to motivate a group of salespeople, don't say, "The salespeople are going to have to really push the boat out this next quarter if the company targets are going to be met." This is far too impersonal, try instead, "We are relying on you to make the difference, you're the ones out there talking to the customers, you know the business. If you can push the boat out for the next quarter, we can reach our targets and we'll all do well at the end of the year." This is much more personal. Note the use of the word 'you'. This is one of the most powerful words in the English language. It makes what you are saying appear relevant to the audience. It makes them sit up and take notice.

KEEP THE NUMBER OF POINTS SMALL

If you try to get too many points across at one time, you run the risk of your audience forgetting them all. Imagine you're just nipping down to the local shops to buy a few things you've run short on during the week. You need bread, milk and cat food. Those three things are relatively easy to remember between here and the shops. But what happens when you are asked to remember a fourth or fifth item? Unless you are blessed with a good memory, it suddenly seems like a mammoth task to memorise them all the way to the shops. The more you try to remember the more likely you are to forget all of the needed items.

Don't expect your audience to remember any more than five points, it is even better if you can keep it down to three.

The Power of Threes

Have you ever noticed how often things in life happen in threes?

- Morning, noon and night.
- Faith, hope and charity.
- The Father, Son and Holy Ghost.
- This, that and the other.
- The sun, moon and stars.
- Tom, Dick and Harry.
- The good, the bad and the ugly.

There is a great rhythm in threes. They add a lot of interest to a presentation when you use them. They add punch, colour and oomph! to your speech.

ACRONYMS AS MEMORY AIDS

Acronyms can be a powerful memory tool – not just for the audience, but for you too. They work best when they have real meaning, like the VHF above. John Townsend talks about three channels, VHF is a channel. This helps to make it memorable for a long time. It is essential that each letter represents the key thought in the concept you want them to remember. One which I find works well for me, when teaching presentation skills, is:

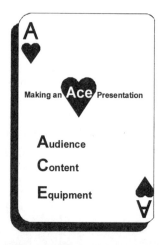

Each key concept is represented in the word ACE. It has the added advantage in that there is a strong visual possibility.

ANALOGIES

Some years ago, I asked a group of participants on one of my courses to make a presentation on 'The Elements of a Good Presentation'. They put together a wonderful presentation using the analogy of building a fire.

- They said that to start a fire, you need a spark, so too with a presentation, you need an opening bang.

- A fire needs three or four main logs or briquettes as a framework. A presentation must have three or four key points or concepts.

- In between these main logs are smaller sticks or newspaper. In the case of a presentation, these are the stories, examples and sub-points.

- The overall feeling you get when you sit in front of a good fire is a warm glow. This should be how you feel when you watch a good presentation.

They brought it to life through a step by step visual build up of the fire, using overhead overlays. It was superb and unforgettable.

Analogies can be drawn from all walks of life; sporting analogies can be particularly powerful. Just make sure your audience has an interest in the analogy you have thought of, otherwise you run the risk of making your points even less digestible instead of helping them to understand.

REMEMBER

DO:

- Use all three communications channels.
- Make everything relevant to your audience.
- Analogies, stories and acronyms as memory aids.

DO NOT:

- Start and finish limply.
- Talk to your audience in the third party.
- Try to tell your audience too much.

Chapter 5

Influencing And Persuading

This chapter will help you to:

- understand that you are selling;
- turn features into benefits;
- use a framework to influence your audience;
- use the best words to sell.

Influencing And Persuading

I remember working with a hotel some years ago. It was a very successful hotel with a strong reputation for customer service. It had been having a problem in the previous few months with it's reservations staff. They were a nice bunch of people who dealt with customer enquiries in a friendly and courteous manner. The problem was that for some time they hadn't been turning enough of these enquiries into sales.

I spent some time listening to the team in action. What they were doing was selling the features of the hotel, not the benefits and to make matters worse, they were selling all the features to all of the customers. In the last chapter, we looked at the importance of relevance. They were breaking this rule blatantly. Features of the hotel included a leisure centre with water slide, jacuzzi and steam room, a variety of restaurants, a bar with live music, all rooms en suite with television and telephone and lots more.

When a hotel is described as above, it sounds sterile and impersonal. Details like this simply give you information, they don't persuade you to buy. If you are to be excited by this hotel, you need to hear what it can do for *you*. The benefits actually tell you what the features can do for you, thereby making them more personal and relevant. A presentation must do the same.

You may be saying to yourself at this point, "But I don't make sales presentations!" Are you sure? When I ask course participants what types of presentations they make they often tell me that they are only there to give information. I don't really believe that. Whenever you stand up in front of a group of people you are always trying to sell something. It may be your company; a product or service; an idea and if you're not selling any of these you are certainly selling yourself.

Most presentations are about selling. You are trying to move your audience from one point of view to another. When you're talking to a group of employees in your department about the last three months results, what are you really trying to do? You are hoping to encourage them to work as hard or even harder for the next quarter, or you certainly should be. If you are a department head talking to the senior management team about what your department has been doing over the past month, you aren't just giving information, you are selling your department and its hardworking staff to the management team.

Whatever else you are doing, you are always selling something. Remember the objectives in Chapter 1? Be clear about exactly what you are hoping to achieve before you start. Do you want to move your audience from one point of view to another, even a subtle change needs you to influence and persuade.

What influences you to buy, or to change your mind? For most people it is usually when they feel there is some advantage for them in changing their way of thinking. You must try to show the audience that it is to their benefit to change their way of thinking or they may not bother.

SELLING BENEFITS TO YOUR AUDIENCE

Let's look at some examples of features, advantages and benefits.

Features

Features are neutral facts, data, information or characteristics which describe what you are selling.

- It will cost £10,000.
- There is a 3-year warranty.
- We have fifteen branch offices, nationwide.

These don't tend to have much impact on a potential buyer. They are too impersonal, too distant and don't easily fit the needs of the audience.

> **WORD TO THE WISE**
> Real benefits of your product, service or idea are much more persuasive than features and advantages.

Advantages

Advantages show how products, services, or your idea can be used.

- Which means it's easy to use.
- So it is the quietest on the market.
- Which means it can be used in any country.

Average salespeople use advantages to sell. They let you go a step further than features and put what you are selling into context for your audience.

Benefits

Benefits show how what you're selling meets an explicit need of your audience.

The best salespeople use benefits. This is why, more than anything else, you need to know your audience and their needs. If you don't know what your audience wants, you won't know what benefits to sell.

Take the hotel example above. The features of a hotel may be:

- leisure centre with jacuzzi, steam room, beauty salon;
- supervised children's playroom;
- romantic dining room;

- baby listening service;
- beside theatres and cinemas;
- luxurious bedrooms with king size, four-poster beds;
- family rooms.

These won't sell the hotel to you by themselves. If you were aware of the advantages of each of these, it may help you to decide. Advantages could be:

- baby-listening service, family rooms and supervised children's playroom will keep children safe;
- because the hotel is beside theatres and cinemas there will be plenty of entertainment;
- romantic dining-room and luxurious bedrooms will mean it's a place suitable for couples;
- leisure centre will provide entertainment for children and relaxation for adults.

They're still a little impersonal though. What will these advantages actually do for you? For a start you'll notice that some will help to sell a weekend away for a couple, others will help to sell a holiday to a family.

You must work out who your audience is. If you're selling your hotel to one category of people, you should only sell the benefits that will influence that group. For couples looking for a romantic weekend away, you could sell them: a lovely, romantic setting with a cosy dining room and luxurious bedrooms with king size, four-poster beds so that you can get away from it all. You can relax and wind down in the leisure centre and soak the working week away in the jacuzzi and steam room. You'll go home ready to face anything. For a family with children, they may be more concerned about the safety and entertainment of the children. But what's really important is what that will do for them. If their kids are being supervised in a playroom they can have peace of mind so that they can relax in the leisure centre or pamper themselves in the beauty salon. If there is a baby-listening service they can go out and enjoy themselves at the local theatre without having to worry about the baby waking up.

In both cases you're selling relaxation but in two different ways. In order to really persuade your audience you must make them feel the benefits, not just know them intellectually. The best presenters will have done their homework on the audience in advance and will be able to sell the benefits to satisfy the needs of any group within the audience.

A STRUCTURED APPROACH TO INFLUENCING

This is a structure that works well for persuasive presentations. There are four simple steps.

1. Create dissatisfaction with the status quo.
2. Paint a vision of a bright future.
3. Reduce the risk.
4. Set out easy, practical steps.

Imagine you're trying the sell the idea of a new telephone system, costing £10,000 for your company to senior management. This could be the bones of your argument.

1. Create dissatisfaction with the status quo
- State number of lost calls through bad connections.
- State number of lost calls through customers having to wait too long.
- Talk about the number of dissatisfied cus-

tomers because of the problems associated with the existing phone system.

- Identify the frustrated feelings of staff from dealing with customers made angry by the phone system.
- Mention that their time is being wasted by angry customers escalating problems to them.
- Describe how the image of the company is suffering due to poor service.
- Show evidence that companies who provide excellent customer service retain more customers.
- And that long-term customers are more profitable than short-term customers.
- Point out how much profit to the company can be lost due to a bad phone service.

Notice that all these are based on fact, either researched within the company or outside. You will also see that some of the above facts will appeal to the 'numbers people' in the audience, others will appeal to the 'feelings people'. All can be made accessible to the visual people through the clever use of charts and graphs.

2. Paint a vision of a bright future

- Remind them that the company wants to make money – that's why they're here.
- Get them to imagine a profitable company, share price rising and with bonuses for everyone.
- Describe the company having high staff morale.
- Say that happy customers will refer the company to their friends and colleagues.
- Point out that there will be less frustration for them – less angry customers escalating their problems to senior management.

- State that there will be more time for them to handle the real issues of the business.
- Describe the possibility of your company having a dynamic, forward-looking image.
- Get your audience to identify with a general feel good factor in the company.

These points are aimed specifically at the audience and will help them to remain interested and be influenced.

3. Reduce the risk

- State that staff will receive comprehensive training so there will be no hitches or teething problems.
- Mention that staff will give out direct dial numbers to all customers so there will be less traffic through the switchboard.
- Talk about having a trial run during the least busy period.
- Say that this system has been tried and tested by companies A, B, C and D.
- Tell the audience that you will arrange an on-site engineer for the first two days to iron out any hitches in the system.
- Promise to run parallel systems over the first six months.
- Tell them that there will be payback within the first two years in saved customers.
- Convince them that a new phone system will enable the company to get a better name in the marketplace.

It is usually necessary to give some sort of cost/benefit analysis when asking anyone to spend money. Companies won't agree to invest unless they can see that the benefits actually will outweigh the cost. This sounds obvious but often when we think something is a good idea we overlook the obvious and assume that our audience will see the benefits as clearly as we do.   Don't ever make this assumption. Benefits need to be laid out explicitly.

4. Set out easy, practical steps

- Ask them to agree on principle that a new phone system is a good idea at today's meeting.
- Tell them that you will get three competitive quotations for the next meeting in a month's time.
- Outline the decision criteria.
- Tell them that all stationery will be printed with the new number(s) by the time the new system is installed.
- Explain that the new system will be up and running in six month's time.
- Make them aware that there will be follow-up training and monitoring.

These steps must show how easy it will be to make this decision. Any ambiguity may hold up the decision.   Try to think ahead to any objections your audience may have to your suggestion and counter them in advance.

This structure can now be made into a very influential and persuasive presentation, adding a punchy start and a memorable ending, punctuated throughout with relevant examples.

Your use of words can also be important. Use too much jargon or stuffy language and you are doomed to fail.   There are some words and phrases which are more persuasive than others.

PERSUASIVE WORDS AND PHRASES

The following twelve words have extraordinary persuasive power.

You	Easy	Guarantee
Money	Discovery	Results
Love	New	Proven
Help	Save	Free
Source: *Department of Psychology, Yale University*		

You will recognise all of these words from their regular use in advertising. This shows that they work. No company would waste advertising money using words that don't persuade.

The word 'you' is probably the most persuasive of all. It connects what you are talking about directly to the listener and makes them believe it is relevant to them.

Below are some opening phrases which can grab attention in a persuasive presentation.[1]

Questions

Did you ever ask yourself...?
Isn't it time you...?
Did you know that...?
Will you be ready for the...?
Wouldn't you like to...?

Statements

If you're like most people, you probably...
It's hard enough to...without having to worry about...
You've probably noticed that...
Just wait until you...

---

1. Bayan, *Words that Sell* (Contemporary Books: 1984).

Challenges
If you're seriously interested in...
Match yourself against...
Join the small handful of people who...
Let your imagination soar...

When you're trying to justify a high price during the presentation
Isn't it worth paying a little extra for...?
Not as expensive as you think...
You probably thought you couldn't afford...

And some closing statements
This is the opportunity you've been waiting for.
In short, you've nothing to lose.
You'll still be able to do it your way – only better!
Try to imagine the alternative.

Try to avoid long, formal words when you could use short, easily understood ones. Unless you're speaking to an academic audience, you will again need to speak in conversational English. Here are some words and phrases that make a presentation sound formal and inaccessible, with some simpler translations.

at this point in time	now
conceptualise	think
continuum	link
impact negatively	worsen
inoperative	doesn't work
interface	meet, work with
normalise	return to normal
optimal	ideal
overriding	major
pursuant to	according to
ramifications	consequences
terminated	finished
with reference to	about
pertaining to	about

owing to the fact that	since
reach a conclusion as to	decide
be cognisant of	know
is of the opinion	believes
make enquiries regarding	enquire

All of the words in the left column are long-winded and need to be shortened so that your audience can stay in contact with you. You'll never persuade your audience if they can't easily understand the message you're trying to get across.

REMEMBER

DO:

- Sell benefits that fit the needs of your audience.

- Remember that you are always selling something.

- Use powerful, persuasive words in your presentations to sell.

- Use a structured approach to influence your audience.

DO NOT:

- Just sell features to an audience.

- Use big words where a little one wise do.

- Put things into the third party – it makes them impersonal.

Chapter 6

Delivering Professionally

This chapter will help you to:

- become aware of your body language and use it well when presenting;
- understand the need for getting good eye contact with your audience;
- use your voice powerfully to really get your message across;
- avoid annoying habits.

Delivering Professionally

Making a presentation is about communicating with your audience. The better you communicate with that group of people the better your presentation will be.

Dr Albert Mehrabian[1] conducted extensive studies on communication of feelings and attitudes, below are some of his findings.

Figure 6.1: Modes of communication and percentage of message

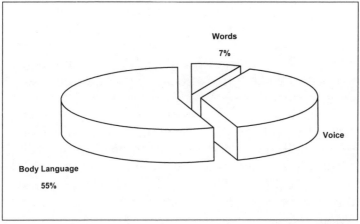

Dr Mehrabian believes that only 7 per cent of the emotional content of the message you send comes across in the words you use, 38 per cent depends on the tone of your voice and a staggering 55 per cent on your body language. These findings may seem a little extreme to some of you, but if you're sceptical,

WORD TO THE WISE
Your body language and voice tone make up a large part of the message you communicate – use them to the full.

---

1. Mehrabian, *Silent Messages* (Wadsworth Publishing: 1981) p. 76.

go and sit in an airport, bar or café for an hour and observe people communicating with other. See just how much information you can get from the body language alone, then move a little closer and hear the voice tones, but without listening to the words spoken, see how much more you can work out. The words, when you finally hear them won't add a huge amount to your understanding.

BODY LANGUAGE

Notice your own body language while you're speaking. Do you stand still while you're talking to a friend or colleague or do you move your hands, arms and feet? Try describing a huge building, a tiny speck or a spiral staircase without moving your hands. Pick common phrases, such as "it's a beautiful day, isn't it?" Try saying it in lots of different ways, using different body gestures, facial expressions and voice tones and see if it comes across differently to others. We all use gestures and facial expressions to get our message across while we're talking to others, but for some reason most of us find it difficult to decide what to do with our hands while we're presenting. We seem to believe that we have to behave differently while we're communicating just because it is a presentation and we're on stage. The best speakers use the same gestures as they use during normal communications. The more natural you look the better. This makes you more believable and credible as a speaker. Some of us also feel we have to stand with our feet in the same place throughout our time on stage. This isn't natural either so why do it?

One of the reasons we have such a problem with our body language is that when we get nervous and the adrenaline starts pumping around our bodies, it makes our muscles slightly more rigid than usual which results in some of our movements appearing robotic. In order to avoid this effect, try shaking out your arms and legs before you come into the room to make a presentation. Excuse yourself for a few minutes and go out to the loo. Stand loosely and fling your arms out in front so that you can feel the muscles in your shoulders tense. Repeat this about five times. You should find your hands are now a little tingly. This means that if you try to use your hands to gesticulate during your presentation, your movements should be natural instead of stilted.

Try the same with your legs. Usually the taller you are the more this is a problem for you. Your knees can lock up and you can end up walking like you're on stilts. Try standing on one leg at a time and shaking out the knee a little. This should help you to relax the muscles in your legs.

There is something about giving presentations that makes us unnatural and rigid. We tend to think that we must behave in a formal manner. We even prefer to stand behind a table or lectern so that we're hidden from the audience as much as possible. This makes us feel safer, but it also takes away much of our power as a presenter because our audience now can't see our body language as easily. You're always better to come out from behind these barriers and connect more closely with your audience.

Facial expressions are also important as a means of communicating a message. When you're having a conversation with a friend or colleague, and they're doing the talking, you watch their face while listening to them. You do this because you get a lot of information from their facial expressions. Your audience does the same during your presentation. They're watching your face to get a large part of the message. If you're smiling they will take one meaning, if you're scowling, they will get another.

Sometimes our faces go blank when we're nervous. This can make the audience believe that you're not interested in what you're saying yourself and it may be harder for them to take your message on board. If you're scowling, they may find you intimidating. Again, you may be scowling because you're nervous. Your facial expressions can so easily be misconstrued by your audience.

Be careful how you stand. If you slouch and lean against a wall with your hands in your pockets, it is likely that your audience will believe that you don't have much respect for them. Similarly, if you drag your feet along the ground while you're walking about and sighing, they may get the same impression.

Make sure you have your hands open towards your audience while you're talking to them, especially if you want them to join in. Some people have a fear of the question time at the end of presentations. One of the fears is that no one will ask a question. If this ever happens to you, take a look at your body language while you're saying, "Any questions?" If you have your arms folded and your feet crossed which is quite common, you have your answer. 7 per cent of you is saying "any questions?", 55 per cent of you is saying, "don't you dare!" No matter what voice tone you use, it isn't enough to tip the balance in favour of the audience feeling comfortable asking questions.

If you really want your audience to join in, you must open your hands towards them, smile encouragingly and speak in a warm tone of voice. (There's more about this in the next chapter.)

EYE CONTACT

There are two reasons why you should work on getting good eye contact with your audience. Firstly, you need to get information from them. If you look at their eyes throughout your presentation, you will know how they're feeling about the different issues that you're talking about. Watch their faces as you try to explain a complicated and complex area and you will know if they're understanding you, or not. If they understand you clearly you will see them smiling and nodding. If they are lost they

> **WORD TO THE WISE**
> Making strong eye contact with each audience member flatters them and enables you to build a good relationship with them during your presentation.

are more likely to have quizzical looks on their faces. This is useful information. Make the most of it.

You may notice that a large number of the group of people in front of you are drifting off, eyes glazed over and sliding down in their chairs. If this happens, stop what you're doing *immediately*. You are boring them. Recap quickly in two sentences and say you'd like to move on to a different area, or suggest a quick break if that's appropriate. Whatever you do, don't continue. This is only wasting their time and yours and they won't forgive you easily. If, however, one person is looking bored and disinterested, don't be disheartened. Maybe that individual had a late night. Be guided by the majority, however they are behaving.

The second reason to make eye contact with your audience is to show them that you're interested in them. Looking at each person in turn will make them feel included and flattered. This will help you to build a good relationship with them. Remember, people buy people. If you want them to buy what you're selling, they must buy you first. They need to like and respect you. The best way to get people to like you is to show you're interested in them. You do this mainly through eye contact. Don't just sweep past their eyes, though. You need to hold the eye contact long enough to actually connect with them. It should be like having a conversation with individual members of the audience.

Some of you may feel a little intimidated when you try to make eye contact with your audience. You must get over this. The problem is that people never see your intentions. They only see that you aren't looking at them and perceive that you aren't interested in them.

Be careful not to miss out on anyone.   This is particularly difficult if the chairs are set out in a U-shape, like around a board room table. It is easy to miss out the people nearest to you. If you don't make a special effort to make eye contact with these people they may feel left out. When people feel left out they may start looking for attention in other ways. This is not always helpful to you, the pre-senter. This is how hostile audience members are born. To avoid creating difficult audience members, ensure you are including everyone.

You may also fall into the trap of looking at one person more often than the others because they appear to be nodding and smiling a lot or because they are the decision maker. The rest of their col-leagues will resent this and again may become hos-tile towards you either during question time or afterwards when you've left and the decision is being made.

If you are working with a large audience, you need to keep moving around so that you can get eye contact with the entire audience, as some will be hidden behind others. The movement will also add interest to your presentation.

USING YOUR VOICE

Your voice is one of your most persuasive features. It can say so much about you and your commitment to what you're saying. I'm sure you've sat through a speech where the presenter spoke in a monotone for twenty minutes and bored the entire audience to tears. The more interesting you can make your voice the easier it will be to listen to. You can use a range of tones, pitches, paces and volumes to add interest. When you are emphasising a point, you can use any of these. If you add the appropriate body language, it can be extremely powerful as a persuasive tool.

If you find you can't easily change your voice, you can try a few solutions. A simple way of improving your voice is to get yourself a large book of fairy stories and some young children, preferably about 6 or 7 years old. Sit them around on the floor. Sit down with them and read the stories using all the voices. Every fairy story has **great big giants and monsters** and *little teeny weeny fairies and elves.* These all have different voices. Just think of the scope you'll have with "Goldilocks and the Three Bears". The reason you should read these to children rather than reading them on your own is this. Children absolutely love adults reading to them using all the daft voices. They smile and roll around laughing when you do this. This will give you the positive reinforcement you need to help you to increase your range of voice tones while you're presenting. Every time you use your increased range, you'll remember the children's smiling faces and know it is a good thing to do.

Another way to help your voice is to do some voice exercises. Here are some simple ones you should do every day to keep your voice in top shape.

Jaw Drop

Let your jaw drop as far as possible, then close the mouth, repeat six times. You should feel sore on either side of your jaw. This will help to correct a stiff jaw.

For Flexible Lips

Repeat ah-oo, ah-oo several times.

Tongue Darting

To correct a lazy tongue, try shooting your tongue out as far and as hard as possible until it is tired. It will then fall naturally into its right position in your mouth. This will ensure you won't get tongue-tied.

Pitch, Pace and Pause

The best exercise for working on pitch, pace and pause is reading aloud as much as possible. Try poetry and prose, modern and old. Find pieces you like and read aloud with enthusiasm. It will have the added benefit of increasing your vocabulary and widen your knowledge of literature you can quote from during your presentations.

Breath Control

Breathe in through your nose. Breathe out with a prolonged hum, or to numbers if you like. Don't continue until you have to gasp for breath, this can do you damage.

Try breathing in for three counts, hold breath for three counts, breathe out for three counts. Repeat, increasing the counts. Both of these exercises will help you to control your breath more easily when speaking.

ANNOYING HABITS

We all have these and they usually get exaggerated when we're nervous. Have you ever noticed that other people tend to pick up a certain word or phrase and use it constantly for a number of months before they let it go and take up with a new one? You probably do this too. You need to find out what word or phrase you repeat. Typical ones are 'basically', 'actually', 'okay', 'right', 'em', 'lo and behold', 'do you know what I mean', 'like' , 'to illustrate my point' and 'for the sake of argument'. There are lots more. If you constantly use the same word or phrase, you may find that your audience becomes distracted and spend most of the time while you're speaking, counting how many times you use your word rather than listening to what you have to say.

Other annoying habits include clicking a pen, fiddling with keys, jingling money in your pocket and scratching yourself in the same place every few seconds. My own personal habit for a while was frantically pacing up and down, not just wandering slowly around. This happened when I got extremely nervous. It got so bad that one of my colleagues told me if I didn't stop she'd nail my foot to the floor. I got the message and stopped doing it. You need to find out what your annoying habit is and eliminate it from your repertoire. Becoming aware of your own words and movements while you're on your feet, and being able to correct the problems while you're still there, comes with time. But at the beginning you will need to rely on your trusted friends and colleagues to let you know what daft things you're up to. Or you could attend a good course on presentation skills where you will get the feedback you need.

REMEMBER

DO:

• Use the full power of your voice.

• Find out what your annoying habits are and eliminate them.

• Make good eye contact with everyone in your audience.

• Use your body language to help express yourself.

DO NOT:

• Stand still with your hands by your sides.

• Alienate audience members by ignoring their eyes.

• Mumble or speak in a monotone.

Chapter 7

Working With The Audience

This chapter will help you to:

- get involvement from your audience;
- handle difficult questions;
- handle questions with ease.

Working With The Audience

INVOLVING YOUR AUDIENCE

You may be thinking to yourself, "Why would I want my audience to get involved in my presentation?" This is a valid question. It will depend entirely on what you are trying to achieve, how you are hoping to achieve it and on your own individual style.

It is difficult for any of us to concentrate on anything for very long. Most of us have an attention span of about twenty minutes. This means that if you're presenting for any longer than this, you will need to add variety to your presentation. One way to add a bit of variety, and keep your audience interested, is to involve them in some way.

Remember in Chapter 4 we discussed using 'Visual, Hearing and Feeling' to help your audience remember what you are saying? Involving your audience in your presentation appeals particularly to the feeling people among them and will add spice and interest to your entire presentation.

Another advantage is that it will help take the spotlight off you for a while. This can work particularly well at the start of your presentation when you are more nervous. If you open your presentation with a question, the audience is now focused on answering your question rather than staring blankly at you waiting for inspiration. You could try asking a question, such as, "How many of you have tried this product before?" This will give you a show of hands. You could go further and try asking a question which individuals in your audience will answer, such as, "How did it work for you?" Hopefully you will get some positive responses.

There are, however, a few rules which you should adhere to if you want this interaction to be suc-

cessful.   Firstly,   never   pick   on
individuals.   If you point out one
person in your audience and ask
them for an opinion on what
you've just said or for their feelings
on a particular issue, it may be

just that moment that he or she has drifted off and
is now mortally embarrassed that they have been
put on the spot.   They will hate you for this.
Secondly, only ask unambiguous questions. It is
very awkward if you ask a question that people
don't understand or aren't sure exactly what you
are looking for.

Thirdly, always reward participants.   Whoever
answers your question and whatever strange
answer they give, don't embarrass them or belittle
them in front of the whole group. Make sure that
whatever answer they give is acceptable, even if it
wasn't what you were expecting.

Sometimes it is better to laugh at yourself than at
an audience member by saying something such as,
"Well I obviously didn't communicate that very well,
sorry about that, let me have another go." Then you
can rephrase the question so that you stand a
chance of getting the right answer. Don't, under any
circumstances, say "No, that's not right, anyone
else?" This will have the result of the person who
answered you feeling bad and everyone else feeling
embarrassed for them and deciding that it is just
too risky to join in as the same might happen to
them.

Whatever the answer you get, you should smile
and look interested. This will make the person who
joins in feel good for doing so. You can add to this
good feeling by repeating the answer out loud to
make sure that everyone hears it or, even better,
writing it on a flip chart or white board. Be careful
here, however, to write their exact words down. If
you change the words they use into words of your

own, it sounds as if you're correcting them. They won't like this. If they have given you a long answer you can ask how would they put that in a few words so that you can best capture it. If they are having trouble with this, you can prompt them. But always make them feel that it is their words and sentiments that are being written down. This makes them feel rewarded.

Another way to reward involvement is to refer back to certain individuals who answered your questions earlier in your presentation. For instance, at the start of your presentation, you might have asked about the uses people put a particular product to. You got five or six answers. If, as you cover the different uses during the presentation, you refer to Joe who has used it for this and Pat who used it for that, it is a powerful way to make these particular audience members feel involved and important. Next time you ask a question, everyone will want to join in so they can get rewarded in the same way.

HANDLING HOSTILE AND DIFFICULT AUDIENCE MEMBERS

Sometimes you don't want to encourage participation. In fact, there are times when you are afraid of your life that certain people will join in. There are a variety of ways to handle these situations. Which one you choose will depend on a few factors. One of these is judging how comfortable you are with handling interaction. Some people love it, others hate it. It will depend on your individual style. It will also depend on how well you know your subject. You may find that audience participation is great on a subject you know well but if you are winging it, you become more uncomfortable. This is quite normal. Remember you don't have to adopt the same style for every presentation. The worst thing you can do with difficult participants is to behave like a victim. You must remain in control and show that they aren't giving you any trouble at all. Where possible, harness their energy and use their willingness to get involved to your advantage. Here are some behaviours which can cause difficulty.

The Know-all

You will often have a know-all in the group, someone who keeps stealing your thunder or answering every single question you ask. The first thing to think about is why they are behaving like this. Often it is because they feel they, not you, should have been asked to make this presentation and they want everyone else in the audience to recognise their superior knowledge of the topic. If this is the case, you need to flatter them. Make a point of saying something like: "Well, we obviously have an expert here, do you mind if we call on you every now and again during the afternoon to help out?" Make sure you smile warmly at them while you say this and look genuinely pleased that they are there. This usually stops them because they have now been recognised as the expert they feel they are and don't have to keep proving it. You usually won't even have to call on their 'expertise', just throw a knowing glance and a smile in their direction every now and again.

The Joker

The joker can sometimes be a handful but can also be great fun if you handle them the right way. The best presentations have energy and a few laughs. The joker can provide these for you. Use their energy and sense of humour to carry the audience through. If they are genuinely funny, encourage them to join in by rewarding their jokes and one-liners. If, on the other hand, they are trying to be smart but the audience just isn't laughing, you can add a tail to their jokes which makes them funny or make some comment about their comments. This can have the effect of the joker thinking they've said something funny and make the rest of the group laugh, so everyone wins. Whatever you do, though, don't put them down and make them feel stupid. The audience should be protected from constant, unfunny wise cracks but the joker shouldn't be ridiculed while you're doing this. You don't have to be the funniest person in the room. Whoever makes the audience laugh is helping your presentation. Just make sure the joker doesn't take over. You must remain in control.

Hostility and Anger

Sometimes you may have to face a group of people who really don't like or agree with what you are saying. Again, remain in control. Don't get sucked into arguing with them. Show respect by letting them have their say. Listen to them courteously. Show understanding by reflecting back the core of what they have said. Don't get defensive. Watch the rest of the audience while your opponent is speaking and while you're speaking and judge whose side they are on. If they are clearly with you, you are in a strong position, so restate what you have said and say you'd be glad to talk to him or her about it afterwards. Then move on. If your opponent keeps coming back on you, the rest of the audience will keep them at bay. You have let them have their say, after all. Now they want to hear what you have to say.

If the audience is clearly on your opponent's side, you must be careful not to put them down in any way, but using logic, evidence and facts, talk your way through your argument and ask them to bear with you until you have put your point across. You will be happy to answer questions when you've fin-

ished, but do ask their permission
before continuing. It would be
unusual for them not to grant this
permission and you will then have
their attention. Show genuine
interest in their points by using
open body language while listening
and warm facial expressions.
Everyone is entitled to their opin-
ion, even if they don't happen to agree with yours.

> **WORD TO THE WISE**
> Don't ever be afraid of audience involvement. Use their energy to add interest to your presentation.

USING BODY LANGUAGE TO CONTROL DIFFICULT AUDIENCE MEMBERS

Whenever you want to get audience participation,
you must use your body language carefully.
Always have open hands towards your audience,
uncrossed legs and a warm smile. This way people
will be encouraged to join in. The only time you
change this rule is when you don't want particular
group members to participate. Imagine you have an
audience member who likes the sound of their own
voice, and jumps in first every time you ask a question. You can control this type of behaviour with
your body language.

Next time you ask a question, hold out a closed
palm towards this person, not in their face like a
policeman but flat, horizontal to the floor. At the
same time, open your other palm towards the rest
of the audience, encouraging participation. This
works like a dream with most people. They won't
even get offended. The reason it works so well is
that the person you are shutting out is not aware
they are being stopped. Only their subconscious
gets the message and they decide themselves that
they would rather not join in this time. If, however,
you do the policeman trick and put your palm flat
towards their face, they will notice and will be high-

ly offended and will more than likely try even harder to take over control from you. So, be careful.

HANDLING AUDIENCE QUESTIONS

One great fear of every presenter is that the audience will ask questions to which they don't know the answers. Never fear, help is at hand. The first thing to remember is that you don't have to know everything. There is nothing wrong in saying, with confidence, that you don't know but that you will find out and come back to them. Another way is to open it to the rest of the group, "Have any of you come across a problem like this before?" Anyone who has will be glad to join in.

Have you ever noticed the way politicians answer questions? They very cleverly start by answering the question they've been asked but then twist the answer around to fit the question they want to answer. You can prepare for question time in advance by using this technique. Work out the questions you are likely to be asked, both the ones you'd like to be asked and the ones you are dreading and work out some good answers. Work out how to side-step some and answer others completely.

Always answer questions concisely, the audience don't want another speech while you're answering a question. This will ensure that you get to as many questions as possible. If you get asked a question you don't understand, put the blame on yourself for not understanding it and ask the questioner to rephrase it. This will save their embarrassment.

Don't ever get defensive during question time. This is a trap that a lot of presenters fall into. You spend twenty minutes putting your argument across and an audience member questions one aspect of it. Your natural, human reaction is to defend your point of view. Resist. If you behave defensively at this time, you may lose the respect of your audience. Instead, take on board the question, listen carefully, understand their point of view and then patiently go over your point again, drawing your questioner into the conversation if you can. If you ask their opinion at this time they will find it harder to argue with you. But always, always, behave warmly towards your questioners. They are then more likely to come around to your way of thinking very quickly. As soon as you argue with them, it will have the opposite effect and they will start to argue back. It is like you're throwing down a gauntlet to them.

For example, you have just made a presentation to your senior management team proposing an investment in a new piece of equipment. The financial controller asks a question about the running cost of the machine. You thought you had covered this aspect very clearly earlier on. It is tempting to answer smartly ("As I said earlier...") or get uppity with your answer ("Obviously this is going to cost a little more, but if we want to get this extra quality, we will have to be prepared to pay for it."), instead, try explaining the answer patiently and when you've finished, you can ask them questions, such as "Does this seem over the top or does it appear to be reasonable value to you?" Be careful here, question time is when the real character of the presenter comes out. Be measured, calm and avoid any confrontations.

So far we've looked at preparing and delivering a good presentation, but even the most carefully prepared and well delivered presentation can lose some of its sparkle if you use the wrong visual aids, so in the next chapter we explore how to add impact to your message by using the right visuals.

REMEMBER

DO:

- Reward all participation.
- Use the energy of the audience to lift your presentation.
- Use your body language to manage audience participation.
- Remain in control at all times.

DO NOT:

- Be afraid of audience participation.
- Ever put any audience member down.
- Get defensive when being questioned.
- Pick on individuals.

Chapter 8

Using Visual Aids

This chapter will help you to:
- choose the right visual aids for your presentation;
- use visuals to help your audience understand you;
- put together really good slides.

Using Visual Aids

Visual aids should be just that, *aids*. All too often presenters rely on their aids too much and the slides take over. They are there to help the audience to understand what you are saying and to help them to remember your key points. Don't fall into the trap of the slides being the only thing the audience engages with during the entire presentation. If your slides are that good, why not just send them the disk and not turn up at all. The truth is that *you* are the most persuasive weapon in your armoury during a presentation, make sure you get the attention you need to do the job. Don't let your visual aids distract from your influencing ability.

So where do you start? First, work out what you are trying to say. What are your main points? What information is absolutely essential for your audience to grasp? Work out what is the best possible way to get this message across to this particular audience.

Sometimes using technology, such as a LCD projected slide-show, is the best method to use, other times it is most definitely not going to do what you need it to do. In fact some audiences will even be intimidated by your use of this type of technology.

The most commonly used visual aids are as follows.

- Flip-charts and white boards.
- Overhead projectors.
- Computer slide-shows using LCD (liquid crystal display) projector.
- Video.

Flip-charts and Whiteboards

These are particularly useful when you are looking for audience participation and want to capture their thoughts. Make sure you write clearly and use large writing. Use a variety of colours and always check the pens beforehand. They often run dry and then create an unprofessional image of you as a presenter. It is always best to carry your own pens around with you as part of your kit. This way you will be certain that they will work well.

> WORD TO THE WISE
> Choose the equipment you use carefully – make sure both you and your audience are comfortable with it.

The main advantage of using either of these aids is that very little can go wrong as neither depends on electricity. It is, however, difficult to make copies of your deliberations using a flip-chart unless they are typed up afterwards. If you feel this is going to be necessary, a whiteboard with a built in copier can be useful. This way you can get a paper copy of your whiteboard with the press of a button within minutes.

When you are writing on either of these tools, don't turn your back on the audience. This will break the eye contact you have built up and harm the relationship you have with them. If you're going to use a flip chart or whiteboard, practise in advance so that you can write by standing to one side.

Overhead Projector

This is probably the most commonly used tool for using visual aids during presentations. It means that you can prepare good visuals in advance and stay in control of the technology relatively easily. You do need a little practise to make sure you're using it well.

All overhead projectors are different so look at the one you are going to use in advance and identify where the switch is so that you're not messing about looking for it when you try to show your first slide. Overhead projectors need power to make them work – it may seem obvious but do check that it is plugged in before you start. Another likely pitfall is the bulb blowing. Most modern projectors have a spare bulb built in which can be changed at the flick of a switch. Check before your presentation that you know how to do this.

When you're using the overhead projector, stand far enough away from it so you're not blocking the screen, but not so far that you have to walk miles every time you want to change a slide. Also stand where you can read from the screen, not from the slide on the overhead projector. You should find a position where you can face your audience at all times but read the screen by just turning your head. Never turn your back on the audience. The reason you read from the screen is this is what your audience can see. If you fall into the trap of reading from the overhead projector itself, it is possible that the image is not being projected onto the screen. I had a lecturer once who used to write equations on the overhead projector and expect us to follow complicated algebra but nine times out of ten it was being projected onto the ceiling. Needless to say, his audience had very little respect for him.

Computer Slide-shows using LCD Projection

These are modern, high-tech and can be very impressive. They can also break down so beware and have a contingency plan in case this happens. They are particularly powerful if you want to show step by step approaches and build up graphics bit by bit. But, a word of warning, they are sometimes used just to impress and the presenter often gets sucked too far into the technology so their presence gets lost completely.

If slide-shows using LCD projection are used

well, they can be brilliant but, because they are so busy, you may spend a lot of time peering into your laptop or at the screen to make sure the right things are showing. You will need a lot of practise to get them right. They are particularly good for large groups, as the image on the screen can be much clearer than that from an overhead projector. If you are used to using an overhead projector and now want to try LCD projection, make sure you try it out in advance. With the overhead projector, you can see the slide you are going to use as you put it on the projector, with LCD projection you won't know what's coming up until you press that button and you may get a surprise.

Do always use a mouse or a remote mouse to change slides, otherwise you'll have to stand still right beside the computer. The remote mouse needs a lot of practise, try this out too. What I find useful is to use the keystrokes for all the functions, such as opening the file, starting the slide show, etc, and use the remote mouse for just going on to the next slide. I would always have a sheet of simple instructions beside me when I present using this technology. These things always seem simple sitting at your desk but when you're panicking in front of a large group of people, simple things like how to open or close the computer package you're using can be a nightmare.

Video

Because videos can encompass the visual, hearing and feeling all in one go, they have a tendency to be remembered more easily than other visual aids. However, the audience didn't come to your presentation just to see a video, so use it sparingly. The best way to use video during a presentation is to show short clips that can be used as the basis of a discussion. This will ensure that the audience watches the video and takes the key messages from it.

Making your Presentation Visual

Using your visual aids for text only is really not making the best use of the tool and is not helping your audience to get the message. Whatever type of aids you use, try to use pictures as much as possible. Remember the saying, "A picture paints a thousand words." It's very true. Using some really simple visuals, which can replace words, make your slides more interesting and have a lasting impression on your audience all at the same time. Some examples are given in Figure 8.1.

Figure 8.1

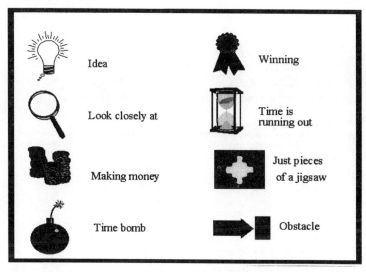

All of the above idea pictures evoke a strong message and are all easily drawn by hand or by using clip art from a computer graphics package. The real trick is to be creative and make the visual do the work for you. Cartoons can work really well for some presenters but the secret to using visual aids is to only use visuals that you are comfortable with.

If you squirm every time you use a particular visual, it isn't for you.

Graphs

When you have figures to present, try to put them in visual format. A sea of figures is very difficult for most of us to understand. A graph showing a trend is much easier. A set of figures showing the sales of ice-cream may look like this:

	1998	**1999**
Jan - Feb	£3,227	£4,556
Mar - Apr	£5,632	£7,782
May - Jun	£25,088	£35,667
Jul - Aug	£27,761	£21,493
Sep - Oct	£11,913	£12,484
Nov - Dec	£13,719	£9,739

For those among us who don't work with figures as a chosen field, we will have to calculate the trend as we read these figures. This is hard work but if these were to be shown graphically, the trend is much more obvious.

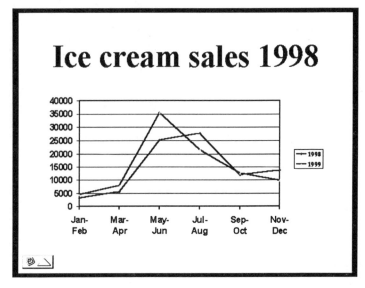

Some of the most professional visual aids are put together using a computer graphics package, such as PowerPoint. This can be used for either overhead slides or LCD projected slide shows.

> **WORD TO THE WISE**
> Keep visuals simple and visual – text is not a visual.

MAKING GOOD SLIDES: 10 SIMPLE RULES

1. **Keep it simple**. Limit your text to bullet points. Keep editing until you have only two or three words per bullet. Never use entire sentences. These take too long to read and will take the attention away from you for too long.

2. **Limit your ideas to one per slide**. Don't try to achieve too much on any one slide as this will make it difficult for the audience to grasp your key point.

3. **Always use a visual where you can**. It will get the message across much quicker and be more memorable.

4. **Create depth in your text by always using bold and shadow**.

> This is ordinary text.
>
> **This is bold and shadowed.**

5. **Use the largest font you can.** 44 point is best, 24 point is the absolute minimum which can be read at a distance.

6. **Keep your background simple**. Don't use fussy backgrounds on your slides just because they

are available. Try to keep them to one plain colour. If you are using a dark background colour with light text, you will need to pick a much darker colour for LCD projection than for over-head projection. This is because there is more light being put through them. If you want to make your background more interesting, try grading it. You can graduate the colour from dark to light in lots of different ways.

7. **Choose your colours wisely**. Different colours evoke different emotional responses. Below is a simple chart.

COLOUR	EMOTIONAL ASSOCIATIONS
Blue	Peaceful, soothing, tranquil, cool, trusting.
Red	Losses in business, passion, danger, action, pain.
Green	Money, growth, assertive, prosperity, envy, relaxation.
White	Neutral, innocence, purity, wisdom.
Yellow	Warm, bright, cheerful, enthusiasm.[1]

Equally important is your text colour. Don't ever use red or green as text colours as there is a large percentage of the population who are colour blind and all that many of them will see is a blur. Use these colours as highlight colours instead.

---

1. Wilder & Fine, *Point, Click and Wow!!* (Pfeiffer & Company: 1996) p. 63.

8. **Try to use serif fonts rather than sans-serif**.
   Serif fonts are those with the 'tails'. Sans-serif
   are those without the 'tails'.

---

d this is serif

d this is sans-serif

We learn to read using serif fonts, we read it in
books and newspapers so are used to it. It is,
therefore, easier and quicker to read than sans-
serif fonts.

9. **Never use capital letters for text**. They are very
   hard to read. If you were to try to read a sentence
   written in capitals and a sentence written in lower
   case, you will notice that the lower case is quicker.
   This again is because we learn to read this way. We
   recognise whole words and phrases at a time.
   When we read capitals, we have to read letter by
   letter and this is a much slower process. You need
   your audience to read quickly so use lower case.

UPPER CASE AND IS SLOW TO READ.

lower case and is much quicker.

One of the reasons we use upper case on slides is
because when we used typewriters, the only way to
make text bigger was to use capitals. Now with
wordprocessing and graphics packages we can
make text stand out by using larger font sizes.

10.**When creating slide shows for LCD projection, you will need to add transitions between
   slides**. These will bring you from one slide to the
   next. Choose the simplest ones. There are a lot of
   complicated, flashy transitions that will distract

your audience from the slides themselves. The simplest ones fade from one slide to another.

You may also want to add sounds to your slide show. Don't have sound on every slide. It gets annoying after a while. Use this sparingly for maximum impact, maybe on one or two selected points.

If you follow these simple rules, you'll be able to make excellent slides for every type of presentation, which will enhance your key points and help to make them memorable.

REMEMBER

DO:

- Use simple visuals – complicated ones distract your audience.

- Practise with your visual aids in advance.

- Check out your equipment before you start.

DO NOT:

- Use technology with which you are uncomfortable.

- Use complicated visuals to impress – they don't.

- Turn your back on the audience while you're using equipment.

Chapter 9

Humour As A Tool

This chapter will help you to:

- see the advantage of using humour in your presentations;
- find the best type of humour for you and your audience;
- find and use suitable humour.

Humour As A Tool

Humour lifts people generally. Did you know that laughter is one of the best stress-busters known to man? The medical profession has been interested in this area for some time now. They have even discovered that laughter can not only reduce stress but also increase your resistance to infection. Just think of the good you can do by adding a little humour into those dry presentations. Laughter really is a great medicine.

Think about how you feel before you start making that presentation. Remember the nerves we talked about in Chapter 1? You are probably highly stressed at this point. Now if you can have a laugh yourself, your stress and panic will ease. Your nerves and those awful symptoms of nerves: shakes, wobbly voice and all the others will abate. Now, if you stand there laughing at your own little joke yourself, the audience will more than likely take offence or wonder what sort of lunatic you are. But if you can get them to laugh with you, now you're on the way to a stress-free presentation.

Remember they may also be nervous. They are wondering what to expect from you. In some cases they are afraid that they won't understand what you're saying, afraid that they are wasting their time. They may also fear that you may pick on them, ask them a question they can't answer and they'll make a fool out of themselves. Giving them a good laugh will reduce their stress levels as well, leaving them to enjoy your presentation and learn from it. It is also a well-known fact that it is easier to learn if you feel safe and are enjoying yourself.

But what happens if you aren't a funny person? You can't even tell a joke successfully to your friends. Luckily, jokes aren't the only way to make people laugh. In fact, I would recommend that you don't use jokes as part of a presentation. For a start, it is far too easy to get them wrong and, if they fall flat, you end up feeling like a total fool. Secondly, they can take away from what you are saying and demean your presentation.

But don't try to tell me that you never laugh or make others laugh. We're all funny at times, sometimes when we don't mean to be. Next time you say something funny and make everyone around you roar with laughter, think for a moment about what you said, how you said it and what was funny about it. Write it down, capture it for use again in a different context. When you've done this for a while, look and see if there is a trend. If there is, you now know how to make your audiences laugh – it's all about finding your own humour, what type of humour you are comfortable with and makes people around you laugh.

There are lots of ways to lighten your presentation without losing your important message.

Cartoons

Cartoons can work extremely well as visuals. If you know anyone who is a good cartoonist, so much the better. The standard clip-art cartoons can be a little tired by now, but if you can find a CD-ROM with cartoons that aren't in constant use, these may be helpful. As with all visuals, make sure the cartoon illustrates the point you are trying to make, otherwise your audience may be falling around laughing but they aren't actually getting the message. A word of warning, if you don't find the cartoons funny, this will come across so don't use them unless you are comfortable with them.

Video Clips

These can be an extremely powerful way of getting audience attention and relieving the tedium of just listening to a speaker. If they are funny clips, so much the better. As with cartoons they must illustrate the point you are making. If you show a funny video clip, it is likely to be the piece best remembered by your audience. You must ensure that they remember *why* you showed it.

Funny Stories

Funny stories are brilliant for lightening up a presentation. If you tell a story about something that actually happened to you it has an added advantage – you won't forget it, with a little rehearsal it will roll easily off your tongue. If you tell a story well, it will appeal to everyone in the audience. If you include facts and figures, visual descriptions and real feelings, you can capture all of your audience and have them waiting, with bated breath, for the punch line. Try telling your story to different people, in different ways and watch the response you get. You will find some stories will be funny no matter which way you tell them, because they are just really funny things that happened. Sometimes, to add extra humour, you can exaggerate the bits you tell against yourself. This will get empathy from your audience and really getting them feeling the way you did yourself when you were in that situation.

Hooks

A hook is a statement or object designed specifically to get attention. We see them every day as headlines in newspapers, as trailers for television programmes or films, or as teasers for advertisements.

Even the evening news programmes use them. Have you ever
noticed how, just before the break,
they announce what's coming up
next? And there is usually a
human-interest story at the very
end. This is the teaser. We have
to wait right through the adverts
and the second half of the news to

> **WORD TO THE WISE**
> Only use humour you are comfort-able with, if you don't find it funny, neither will your audience.

see what it was about. Clever, isn't it?

So how about hooks in presentations? Try thinking about what is the most unusual, exciting, dra-
matic, interesting or humorous part of your subject.
See if you can reduce this to one sentence – if you
can, you have a hook. But you must make sure
that your hook helps to bring this particular audience towards the objective you have set for yourself.

I'm sure, like me, you'll often think of great ideas
for hooks and stories, which are really relevant
when you aren't trying to prepare for a presentation
only to find that when you really need one, you can't
think of a thing. To help me get over this, I keep a
little red book with me for jotting down ideas that
occur to me when I least expect them. This little
book is invaluable as a source for ideas for these
stories and hooks. One area in which I teach often
is customer service. You can imagine the number of
examples I come across every day of interesting service (whether good or bad) but when I need them
most, they can be a bit illusive. So I have got into
the habit of jotting them down as I come across
them so that next time I need an example – it's just
sitting there waiting for me.

Creating Humour

The most difficult part of using humour is to have
an idea in the first place. How can you add humour
to your subject? After all, it's boring, isn't it? And

even if you did think of a funny story, how can you possibly get it across, because you're not a clown, it is supposed to be a serious presentation. You want the audience to take it seriously, don't you? Now I'm not suggesting for a minute that you are so funny that the audience is rolling around in the aisles, that wouldn't help you at all, but I am suggesting a subtle humour that will lighten the presentation from being dull and dreary to more exciting, passionate and funny.

One of the best ways to think of the funny side of your topic is to have some sort of a brainstorming session with a group of friends, family or colleagues. People who don't know much about your subject can more easily see the funny side. Don't do this in a formal way, but when you meet a group of people, throw out the subject and see what funny remarks or stories come out. You'll be surprised how easily people think of these funny ideas and stories when they're not under pressure.

This has the added advantage of giving you more courage to deliver them when there are a group of people who think it's good, funny stuff. Most of us retreat into the normal, boring, formal way of making presentations because its safe – it may not be interesting to the audience, but at least its safe. We have to force ourselves out of this mould. We have to find the more interesting and brave way to put our message across. There's an old saying that "you can't make an omelette without breaking eggs". This is very true of presentations. Sure, if you want to take the safe option and continue to make safe, passable presentations, go ahead and do it. But if you want to make really good presentations that people will actually listen to and take notice of, you will have to break those eggs and try some new things out. Humour is a wonderful way to ensure that your audience will listen to you. After all, they are now having fun.

Apart from brainstorming with friends, there are some other great sources. Books and magazines, such as *Bits and Pieces*, published fortnightly by The Economics Press Inc., or *The Executive Speaker*, published monthly by The Executive Speaker Co., are invaluable sources of interesting facts and information which are great for presentations. There are also lots of books of humorous quotations, funny poems, books of cartoons – all these will give you some core ideas which you can explore and treat them with your own brand of humour.

Avoid off-colour humour or anything that is aimed at any particular group of people. Stand-up comics can get away with it in a nightclub or on the television but at a business presentation, it is likely to go down like a lead balloon. Don't say anything that may even remotely offend, particularly if you're trying to be funny. People don't like to have fun poked at them or to be laughed at. Usually the best target for a laugh is you. At least you know you can take it. You should also be aware that different cultures laugh at different things. A topic or phrase that is uproariously funny to one culture may be downright offensive to another. Do your homework beforehand and make sure you know the culture you are presenting to.

DELIVERING HUMOUR

You must feel confident when you're delivering the funny bits, if you look nervous and afraid that it will flop, it will. Be animated, pull the necessary faces, use all the voices, this will make the story so riveting that the audience will get sucked in and hear the moral at the end. Don't ever apologise in advance for telling a story just in case it doesn't come across as funny. A good, funny story will work well even if the audience doesn't laugh. If you do get to the end of a story and there is only a polite titter from one or two people, you can make it funny for everyone with a remark, (such as, "Well you obviously had to be there" or look straight at the audience, and say quietly "You know, you really have great self control" or "My mother *really* liked that one"). You may not feel comfortable using one of these lines, but if you do, they can be extremely funny and can save you from a lot of embarrassment. But, as with all humour, only use it if it feels okay to you.

Always rehearse your funny stories, hooks, or whatever you are going to use, in advance. The best presenters will look as though the story has just occurred to them. This is not usually the case. Good presenters rehearse their entire presentation, but pay particular attention to the stories that sound like they're being told 'off the cuff'. This is because a story or joke if it is told badly can be a disaster. If you forget to tell an important bit at the start and get to the end and nobody knows what you're talking about, you are sunk. Then you have to say something like, "Well, I should have told you at the start...". Of course, if you are good at delivering stories, this won't be a problem, this will actually add to the humour of the situation – because you are laughing at yourself. But if you get embarrassed when you make a mistake, the audience will get embarrassed too and your humour just won't work.

REMEMBER

DO:

- Remember that laughter can reduce stress.
- Have a few 'saver' lines ready in case your humour doesn't work.
- Be brave – don't always play safe.
- Get others to help you to be creative.

DO NOT:

- Use humour unless you are comfortable with it.
- Apologise for your humour in advance.
- Use off-colour humour.

Chapter 10

Avoiding Pitfalls

This chapter will help you to:

- pull it all together;
- manage your environment;
- handle problems when they do arise.

Avoiding Pitfalls

PULLING IT ALL TOGETHER

Just as in a good presentation, a book on presentation skills needs to summarise the key points at the end. So here is a 10-point plan for making brilliant presentations.

1. Set a clear objective

Know what you want to achieve and what you want to have in your audience's head when they leave the room. Be aware of what action you want them to take as a result of your presentation. Write it down on a sheet of paper and refer to it often while you're preparing.

2. Know your audience

Find out all you can about them. Know what interests them, what they like, what turns them on. Find out what they know already about your topic so that you can tailor your presentation to the exact group of people who will be there.

> **WORD TO THE WISE**
> The secret to making really good presentations is to prepare well. Always give yourself enough time to do this properly.

3. Prepare your content selectively

Only include content that will bring this particular audience towards the objective you have set. Leave everything else out. It is not relevant. It doesn't matter how interesting you find it. If it doesn't fit the brief, be brave and leave it out.

4. Choose your equipment carefully

Make sure the type of visual aid you are using enhances your message, and does not take away from it. Ensure it is suitable for your audience and that it won't intimidate them. You don't want to come across as too smart. On the other hand, if you are working in an industry that is highly technical, using high-tech equipment will be expected of you. Be sure you are comfortable using the equipment you choose to present with.

5. Find a way to capture ideas and information as you think of them

Try writing down your ideas as they occur to you and keeping them in an envelope on the corner of your desk so it is all together when you need it. Work out where your creative places are. Most of us find it difficult to have unusual or creative ideas sitting at our desks. It is more usual to have our best ideas when we're relaxed and not trying to think.

6. Arrange your material carefully

Pay special attention to the start and finish of your presentation. If you start in an interesting way, your audience will want to hear more. It will also help to calm your nerves for the rest of your presentation. The last few minutes of your presentation will be remembered most by your audience so make sure you summarise well and include your objective in your ending so your audience will be in no doubt as to what they need to do as a result of the presentation. Find ways to help your audience to understand and remember your key points by using acronyms, hooks, stories, analogies, examples and all three communication channels.

7. Put together your visual aids

Avoid using too much text. Pictures are more powerful. Any text you use should be large enough for the audience to read easily and in lower case. Always get someone else to read through your slides in advance. You won't be able to see your own mistakes easily. Do this in plenty of time in case you want to make changes and corrections.

8. Rehearse, rehearse, rehearse

The best presentations are well rehearsed. Always run through your presentation at least once using all your visual aids and props. Try to rehearse in the place you are going to present or at least in a similar venue. Don't run through your final rehearsal sitting at your desk, things are much different when you're standing up with your equipment beside you. Work out contingencies for anything that could go wrong in advance of the presentation. This way you won't be thrown as much when they happen.

9. Deliver professionally

Be aware that nerves are important for making a good presentation but be able to manage the downside of the jitters. Knowing that you can manage and hide your nerves from your audience will help to settle you down. Be ready with a good, strong opening and deliver it with confidence. Work out, in advance, where you are going to stand, where you will put your notes and slides and how to work the equipment.

Don't have pens, paper or anything else in your hand while you are presenting, it will prevent you from using your body language successfully. Maintain good eye contact with everyone in your audience throughout and keep your voice interesting by using the full range of tones and volumes. Use body language and rewards to manage audience interaction and answer questions honestly and concisely.

10.Review each presentation afterwards

Note what went well and what you should change for next time. Ask a trusted colleague for feedback if you can and keep learning. Every time you make a presenta-tion, you can make a better one. Remember presenting is a learned skill.

MANAGING YOUR ENVIRONMENT

A good presentation can be ruined by an inappropriate or unmanaged environment. Your presentation may be very interesting but your audience may still go asleep

> **WORD TO THE WISE**
> Don't leave any-thing to chance – try and think in advance of all the things with which you may have a problem, and solve the prob-lems before they happen.

because the room is stuffy or too warm and the chairs uncomfortable. A little time spent ahead of the event can pay enormous dividends. Unfortunately, you can't always manage the envi-ronment, for instance, when you're presenting on the premises of a client or potential client, but at least thinking about some of these elements in advance can help. Here's a checklist of useful things to look at beforehand.

Room Layout

When we look at an empty room it can often seem enormous but when you start filling it with chairs and tables you will be amazed at just how small it becomes. You will obviously need a larger room if you intend having desks for your audience. Remember you will need a good amount of space for yourself at the top of the room so that you can move about without being on top of your audience.

The best room layout for presenting is one where you can see all of your audience at the same time. A U-shape is preferable for a small or medium num-ber, whereas some sort of auditorium with tiered seating can be useful for a large group. The most difficult layout to work with (but unfortunately the most often used) is a room with an unmoveable large board room table in the middle of it with your audience seated around it. This puts a barrier straight away between you and them and makes your job more difficult. But if that is where the presentation has to be held, then you have to live with it. Try to make a space for yourself where you can move around and maybe use a side table for your notes. Encourage your audience to move away a little from the table so that they will be more comfortable.

If you are using a room with an open U-shape set-up, make sure you have plenty of empty space for yourself in the middle. Don't get trapped behind a table. Find a small table for your overhead projector or your laptop so that you aren't stuck behind another barrier.

Avoid podiums and lecterns where you can. Again, they act as a barrier. In other words, the less there is between you and your audience, the better. If you are using a hotel or conference centre for your presentation, send them a layout plan in advance and indicate which end of the room you want everything to be. You'd be surprised at the different interpretations of your telephone instructions. Half an hour before you start to present is not the time to discover that they got the wrong end of the stick and all the furniture and equipment has to be moved.

Ventilation and Lighting

A warm, stuffy room is a nightmare for you and your audience. Always check where the controls are for the air-conditioning, heating system or windows before you start. Try out your visual aids before anyone else arrives. This is the time to discover that your slides don't show up because the light at the front of the room is too bright. Find out how to change this now. Sometimes, in hotels, the

light switches are in a different room or in a cup-
board and this can cause embarrassment in front of
an audience if you can't find them.

Noise

Always ensure when you're arranging to use a room
for a presentation that you will not be disturbed by
noises from a nearby kitchen, bar, function room or
lift, particularly when you're working in a hotel.
Similarly you need to check that they won't be cutting the grass, cleaning the windows or using a
pneumatic drill right beside where you'll be working. I worked in a conference room in the front of a
hotel some years ago when, all of a sudden in the
middle of the afternoon, we got a 15-minute rendi-
tion of some tune being played extremely loudly on
the bagpipes right outside our window. The piper
was there to pipe all the guests in for a wedding.
Not wanting to spoil the happy couple's big day, we
took our tea break a little early but now I check this
sort of thing out beforehand.

Power Sockets

If you're bringing any equipment with you, it always
safer to have a four-way plug board with a long lead
as part of your kit. This way you won't have a problem with moving equipment around or setting up
two or three pieces of equipment at the same time.

Interruptions

Check that any phones in the room you are using are
switched off and that there is a 'do not disturb' sign
on the door. You should talk to the receptionists, the
porters or conference organisers to make sure that
the presentation will not be disturbed once it starts.
Make sure you know when and where tea, coffee and
lunch breaks are to be held, otherwise you may get a
knock on the door at a critical moment and a porter

arriving with a tray of rattling cups and steaming pots of tea and coffee. There's nothing more distracting to an audience than to get the waft of hot scones straight out of the oven and the smell of French coffee. You may find they lose interest in what you have to say very quickly.

Flip-chart Pens

Always, always bring your own. Never trust anyone to provide you with what you are expecting. You would be amazed at what some conference centres will give out for poor, unsuspecting presenters to write with. Flip-chart pens should be part of your standard kit. You can use a flip-chart if your other equipment breaks down by writing key words and drawing simple diagrams.

Technicians

Have the name and number of a good audio-visual technician with you just in case of breakdowns. The fact that you have a back-up will help your confidence in the equipment even if you never have to use it.

WHEN THINGS GO WRONG

When you are making presentations, things will go wrong. They always do just as they do in just about everything else you do. Have you ever gone through a day at work, doing your usual job, when nothing at all has come unstuck, when nothing has gone wrong and you haven't made a mistake? If you have, you're a very lucky person. Most of us come up against problems constantly but they don't throw us. But when these same problems happen when we're presenting they can cause us to panic. The main thing to remember is you're not infallible – nobody is. Your audience does not expect you to be perfect. In fact, if you were perfect, your audience would probably not like you as this would make you a little inhuman.

Expect things to go wrong, plan contingencies for when they do and don't get rattled and you will find presenting much easier. It's what you do to get out of your dilemmas while you're presenting that is of much more importance and interest to your audience than the fact that you made the mistake in the first place.

Learn to laugh at yourself and your mistakes. Get the audience to join in. Never blame anyone else. I hate to see presenters standing in front of an audience blaming their secretaries for spelling mistakes, technicians for equipment breakdowns or conference organisers for not giving them enough time to explain their topic well enough. These are *your* responsibilities. An audience will not like you if you try to blame others. Just make sure you check everything in advance.

Have a back-up of your notes, slides, know who to ask when you're in trouble, know where the toilets are and relax.

Enjoy yourself – presenting is fun. You get a great buzz when it goes well and if you follow the tips in this book and get plenty of practise there is a very good chance that it will. Good luck, and, to use an acting expression...break a leg!

REMEMBER

DO:

- Have contingency plans for as many potential disasters as possible.

- Check out your venue in advance and know how to work all the controls.

- Relax and enjoy yourself – presenting can be fun.

DO NOT:

- Ever blame anyone else for problems

- Expect to be perfect.

- Leave anything to chance.

Further Resources And References

Further Resources And References

BOOKS AND NEWSLETTERS

Richard C Brandt, *Flip Charts - How to Draw Them and How to Use Them* (San Diego: Pfeiffer Co.) 1986.

Margaret Parkin, *Tales for Trainers – Using Stories and Metaphors to Facilitate Learning* (London: Kogan page Ltd) 1998.

John Townsend, *The Business Presenter's Pocketbook* (Alresford: Management Pocketbooks) 1985.

Lily Walters, *Secrets of Successful Speakers – How you can Motivate, Captivate and Persuade* (New York: McGraw-Hill) 1993.

Jean Westcott & Jennifer Hammond Landau, *A Picture's Worth 1,000 Words – A Workbook for Visual Communications* (San Diego: Pfeiffer Co.) 1997.

Claudyne Wilder & David Fine, *Point, Click and Wow – A Quick Guide to Brilliant Laptop Presentations* (San Diego: Pfeiffer Co.) 1996.

Bits and Pieces published fortnightly by The Economics Press Inc., Fax: +44 (0)1727 844388; e-mail: 100660.2061@compuserve.com

The Executive Speaker published monthly by The Executive Speaker Co., Fax: Ohio 00-1-937-294-6044; e-mail: mail@executive-speaker.com;
Website: www.executive-speaker.com

COURSES

Presentation Skills courses run by Lynda Byron at the Irish Management Institute, Sandyford Road, Dublin 16.
Telephone/Fax: (01) 295 5150
E-mail: Byronl@imi.ie

Presentation Skills
An intensive 2-day course, run monthly from September to June. The emphasis is on building confidence and preparation.

Advanced Presentation Skills
An intensive 2-day course, run bi-monthly. The emphasis is on impact and delivery.

Making Powerful Presentations
Links the technology of PowerPoint with the skills of presentations. It is run twice each year for two and a half days and teaches participants to both put together excellent presentations using PowerPoint and deliver them successfully.

* All of these courses can be run on a company specific basis or tailored to the specific needs of the group.